ON ASCETICAL LIFE

ST VLADIMIR'S SEMINARY PRESS
Popular Patristics Series
Number 11

The Popular Patristics Series published by St Vladimir's Seminary Press provides readable and accurate translations of a wide range of early Christian literature to a wide audience—students of Christian history to lay Christians reading for spiritual benefit. Recognized scholars in their fields provide short but comprehensive and clear introductions to the material. The texts include classics of Christian literature, thematic volumes, collections of homilies, letters on spiritual counsel, and poetical works from a variety of geographical contexts and historical backgrounds. The mission of the series is to mine the riches of the early Church and to make these treasures available to all.

Series Editor
BOGDAN BUCUR

Associate Editor
IGNATIUS GREEN

* * *

Series Editor
1999–2020
JOHN BEHR

On
Ascetical Life

ST ISAAC OF NINEVEH

translated by
MARY HANSBURY

ST VLADIMIR'S SEMINARY PRESS
CRESTWOOD, NEW YORK

LIBRARY OF CONGRESS CATALOGING-IN-PUBLICATION DATA

Isaac, Bishop of Nineveh, 7th cent.
    [Ascetical homilies. Homily 1-6. English]
    On the ascetical life / St Isaac of Nineveh; translated from the Syriac
by Mary Hansbury.
        p.   cm.
    Includes bibliographical references.
    ISBN 0-88141-077-2
    1. Asceticism—Early works to 1800. 2. Mysticism—Early works to 1800.
3. Nestorian Church—Doctrines. 4. Orthodox Eastern Church—Doctrines.
I. Hansbury, Mary. II. Title.
BR65.I653I83   1989   89-38492
248.4'7—dc20   CIP

translation copyright © 1989 by

ST VLADIMIR'S SEMINARY PRESS
575 Scarsdale Road, Crestwood, NY 10707
1-800-204-2665 • www.svots.edu

First printed in 1989

ISBN 0-88141-077-2
ISBN 978-0-88141-077-8
ISSN 1555-5755

PRINTED IN THE UNITED STATES OF AMERICA

Contents

Introduction 7

First Discourse 25

Second Discourse 33

Third Discourse 43

Fourth Discourse 63

Fifth Discourse 81

Sixth Discourse 101

INTRODUCTION

Life and Times

Little is known of Isaac's life. Only two brief references give details. One is in the *Book of Chastity* of Isho'dnah, from the early ninth century.[1] The other is by Rahmani, take from a fifteenth century MS. in Mardin.[2] Both texts say that Isaac was a native of Beth Katraye on the Persian Gulf. After being instructed in Scripture and scriptural commentaries he became a monk and a teacher near his home. The Nestorian Patriarch George noticed Isaac during a pastoral visit and took him back to Mesopotamia with him. George eventually consecrated Isaac bishop of Nineveh (*ca.* 660-680) at the monastery of Beth Abhe. After only five months as bishop, Isaac asked to withdraw and to live as an anchorite in Bet Huzaje. Eventually, he went to the monastery of Rabban Shabur in Iran, near the Persian Gulf. Here he studied Scripture so much that he became blind and had to dictate his writings, which explains certain difficulties of his style. He died at an advanced age and was buried in Rabban Shabur.

---

[1] J. B. Chabot, "Le Livre de la chasteté, composé par Jésusdenah, Evêque de Basrah," in *Mélanges d'Archéologie et d'Histoire* 16 (1986) 277-278.

[2] I. E. Rahmani, *Studia Syriaca* (Lebanon: Charfet Seminary, 1904), p. 33.

The seventh century was characterized by political up-
heaval and transformation, as well as by division and
change within the Church.[3] In the seventh century, the
Sasanian empire came to an end after five hundred years.
By this time, the shape of Roman Syria had also changed
dramatically. After the last Seleucid king was deposed,
Syria had become a Roman province in 64 B.C., to
Rome's significant commercial gain. Thereafter, East Syria
became the battle-ground between Rome and Persia. East
Syrians were Semitic, therefore foreign to both Rome and
Persia. A small, indigenous population had little chance
between such powerful neighbors. To understand East
Syrian Christianity during its first six centuries, it is important to remember that behind synods, bishops, and
theological disputes cities were burning. Even the Persian
martyrs must be understood in this Roman-Persian context. While the Roman Empire was pagan, the Persian
king had little reason to persecute Christians; on the contrary, Persia protected them against her enemy. But when
the empire became Christian, Shapur considered Christians as traitors. Under Shapur II, Persia had more martyrs
than any other part of the Christian world. The Roman
Martyrology lists 9,000 martyrs, and Sozomen 16,000.
Ardashir, Shapur's brother, continued the carnage, as did
Yazdgard I, until the edict of toleration in 409.

There was a temporary halt in the Roman campaign
after the death of Julian (363) and again after the treaty
of Theodosius I in 389, which divided Armenia. But
violence again became intense in 488 when the Persians
invaded Roman Armenia. Turn of the century Byzantine
Syria is perhaps best documented in *The Chronicle of
Joshua the Stylite,* a carefully written account of the

---

[3] See S. P. Brock, "Christians in the Sasanian Empire: a Case
of Divided Loyalties," in *Syriac Perspectives on Late Antiquity*
(London: Varorium Reprints, 1984).

Persian war of Anastasius.[4] By 629, the Persians agreed to give up all Byzantine territory; but there was no lasting gain to the Byzantine empire, for neither side realized how close the Arabs really were. Finally, the Arabs conquered Syria and Babylonia in 636. Under Islamic rule, the fifth-century controversies concerning the nature of Christ became less acute, although the division of Syrian Christians into opposing communions remained: Chalcedonians, West-Syrian Monophysites, and Eastern-Syrian Nestorians. Ironically, good relations continued between Muslims and East Syrians at least until *ca.* 647. Some Muslims felt that the beliefs of the East Syrians were closer to Islam than were the beliefs of the Monophysites. Mohammed himself had a special fondness for East Syrians, since it was apparently a Nestorian priest who had prophesied the mission of Mohammed.[5]

At this time of great internal and external tension for the Syrian church, Iso'yaw III of Adiabene began his ecclesiastical career as bishop of Nineveh in 638. He eventually became one of the three most important patriarchs of East Syrian Christians, together with Timothy in 780 and Iso'bar Nun, Patriarch from 823-828 and an important exegete.[6] Iso'yaw figures in the history of

---

[4]W. Wright, tr., *The Chronicle of Joshua the Stylite* (Cambridge: Cambridge University Press, 1882).

[5]"East Syrian" is a term frequently used to describe the Persian church rather than "Nestorian." The christology of Nestorius is really not at issue in East Syrian theology, at least in its ascetical writers such as Isaac. Macomber maintains that not even the christology of Nestorius as refracted in Theodore of Mopsuestia is "central or essential" to the theological synthesis of East Syrians, even though "officially adopted by the Church of Persia." See W. F. Macomber, "The Theological Synthesis of Cyrus of Edessa, an East Syrian Theologian of the Mid-Sixth Century," *Orientalia Christiana Periodica* 30 (1964) 5.

[6]On the role of the Patriarch, see W. F. Macomber, "The Authority of the Catholicos Patriarch of Seleucia-Ctesiphon," in

Syriac theology at many levels: exegesis, liturgy, theology and letter-writing. Primarily, he compiled the *Hudra,* one of the chief liturgical books in the Nestorian tradition. After the *Syndicon,* the *Hudra* is considered to be the most important source for understanding the Syrian theological synthesis. Among the texts of its music is some of the most beautiful poetry in the early Church. This poetry also gives a good insight into popular piety, since the liturgy functioned as catechesis for the Syrian Christians. In addition, there are letters of Iso'yaw which reflect important moments in the religious tension of that time. In one letter, he speaks of going down to Tabrit, "the great city of the heretics," to do battle with the Mono-physites.[7] Just prior to his death, he chose as successor George of Kaphra, whom he loved greatly because of his wisdom, learning, and humility. He had personally selected George from the ranks of the monks at Bet'Abhe in order to prepare him for ecclesiastical service.

When he died at the age of eighty, Iso'yaw passed the patriarchate on to George, who had been named bishop of the Arabs at Akoula in 636. In addition to his pastoral and administrative duties, George translated Aristotle's *Organon* and commented on it. Thus he was one of many translators of Greek works into Syriac. These, from the fifth century, mark the beginning of the return of Greek thought to the West by means of Arabs who learned it from the Syrians.[8] Finally it was George who consecrated Isaac bishop of Nineveh.

Isaac was born in Bet Qatraye, near present-day Bahrain, an area rich in pearls and also a trade route to India.

---

1 Patriarcati Orientali nel primo millennio, Orientalia Christiana Analecta 181 (Rome, 1968).

[7]The Patriarchal letters of Iso'yaw are in: R. Duval, ed. and tr., *Liber epistularum,* CSCO 64, Ser. 2 (Louvain, 1905).

[8]See De Lacy O'Leary, *How Greek Science Reached the Arabs* (London: Routledge & K. Paul, 1964).

In the sixth and seventh centuries, several other significant writers of the East Syrian tradition lived in Bet Qatraye: Abraham b. Lipeh, Ahob of Qatar, Dadisho of Qatar, and Gabriel of Qatar. Their writings form part of the "stupendous spiritual literature" produced by the early Syrian Church.[9] It was Christianity which, for various political and ecclesial reasons, remained insular: it had its own liturgical life, hierarchy, dogmas, and discipline. Because of its strengths, it was able to survive persecution, and was even able to reach as far as central China in an important and inspiring missionary expansion in 638 AD.[10]

Something more should be said about Isaac's motive for leaving the episcopate after only five months. The hints available seem to indicate that the problem was theological. One of the biographical notations mentioned above indicates that he resigned "for a reason known to God." The other reference, by Isho'dnah, suggests that there was jealousy surrounding the person of Isaac: "He wrote three things which were not accepted by many. Daniel rose against him on account of what he had said . . . I believe that jealousy awakened against him."[11] Another hint appears in the ninth century in the treatise of Ibn as-Salt, compiled in Arabic from the Syriac writings of Isaac.[12] In his introductory remarks, as-Salt alludes to the controversy surrounding Isaac and concludes that

---

[9]See Introduction to the Italian translation of St Isaac: M. Gallo and P. Bettiolo, tr., *Discorsi Ascetici* (Rome: Citta Nuova, 1984).

[10]For archeological and textual evidence of this expansion see, P. Y. Saeki, *The Nestorian Monument in China* (London: S.P.C.K., 1916).

[11]Daniel bar Tubanitha was a bishop at Bet Garmai in the seventh century.

[12]P. Sbath, tr., *Traités religieux, philosophiques et moraux, extraits des oeuvres d'Isaac de Ninive par Ibn as-Salt (IXe siècle)* (Cairo, 1934).

the problem is Isaac's insistence on the primacy of mercy. In fact, the writings of Isaac contain constant reminders of the love one should have for mercy, which he sees as the foundation of adoration and humility:

> And what is a merciful heart? It is the heart's burning for all of creation, for men, for birds, for animals and even for demons. At the remembrance and at the sight of them, the merciful man's eyes fill with tears which arise from the great compassion that urges his heart. It grows tender and cannot endure hearing or seeing any injury or slight sorrow to anything in creation. Because of this, such a man continually offers tearful prayer even for irrational animals and for the enemies of truth and for all who harm it, that they may be guarded and forgiven.[13]

Mercy in itself can be unsettling to self-righteous believers, but perhaps not enough to warrant ecclesial censure. But for Isaac, mercy was carried to the extent that it includes final salvation for all creation, including demons. This Origenist tendency was repeatedly censured by the Syrians, both Nestorians and Monophysites.[14]

Perhaps this merciful heart of Isaac, brought to perfection in the division and upheaval of seventh-century Persia, is precisely what draws the modern mind. So many persons throughout the world are attracted to Mar Isaac. Through his writings, he may be able to offer consolation to a modern society not unlike seventh-century Babylonia in its political upheaval and crisis in faith.

---

[13]See P. Bedjan, ed., *Mar Isaacus Ninivita, De Perfectione Religiosa* (Paris-Leipzig, 1909), p. 507.

[14]See A. Guillaumont, *Les 'Kephalia Gnostica' d'Evagre le Pontique* (Paris: Editions du Seuil, 1962), pp. 333-337.

Phenomenology

The basic pattern of Isaac's monastic anthropology is threefold. This pattern is inherited from John of Apamea and is typically Syrian, though derived from St Paul. Later, this same tripartite division, through a Greek translation of Isaac's *Ascetical Discourses,* had a major influence on all of Byzantine spiritual literature.

Pseudo-Dionysius speaks of the state of the one being transformed: purification, illumination, and perfection or union. Origen and Evagrius concentrate on the practice conducive to this transfiguration: *praxis,* natural contemplation, divine vision. For Isaac the perspective is different: the way of the body, the way of the soul and the way of the spirit.

In the first stage, one begins with a total preoccupation and involvement with passions and moves toward God by means of bodily works. "The passions are: love of riches; amassing of possessions; the fattening of the body, from which proceeds carnal desire; love of honors, which is the source of envy; administration of government; pride and pomp of power; elegance; popularity, which is the cause of ill-will fear for the body."[15] The works of the body by which one moves toward God are: fasting, vigils, psalmody.

During the second stage of the way toward God, the struggle is against thoughts foreign to the nature of the soul. "We believe that God has not made his image subject to passion."[16] Isaac's tripartite schema reflects anthropology more than chronology, but this movement toward purification does occur in two successive moments: first a turning from created objects to the contemplation of God's wisdom; second a transformation from within:

---

[15]See Trans., 2nd Disc., #30.

> For when outside waters do not enter into the
> fountain of the soul, its natural waters spring up—
> wondrous thoughts they are, which are continually
> being moved toward God.[17]

These new thoughts reflect biblical categories: the coming
day of the Lord; God's providence (*oikonomia*); and
his solicitude. The fulfillment of this second stage, in its
quest for purity, is limpidity. Purity is the means by which
one arrives at limpidity of heart, *shafyut lebba*. This
transparency is characterized by a total openness of the
soul to the future hope. The term for limpidity, very
frequent in East Syrian literature, also has roots in
Targumic material, as do other aspects of Syriac theology.[18]
    Concerning the final stage Isaac says:

> As among ten thousand persons hardly one will be
> found who has fulfilled the commandments ap-
> proximately and what pertains to the laws, and
> who has been found worthy of limpidity of soul,
> so only one among many will be found worthy of
> pure prayer by means of much vigilance and [be
> able] to break this boundary and also be found
> worthy of this mystery. Not many are found worthy
> of pure prayer, only a few. But as to that other
> mystery which is beyond it, hardly one will be
> found in each generation who has drawn near to this
> knowledge by the grace of God.[19]

Isaac's reticence in speaking about the third stage is

---

[16]See Trans., 3rd Disc., #5.

[17]See Trans., 3rd Disc., #2.

[18]For the importance of limpidity of heart for "God's self-
revelation to humanity," see S. P. Brock, "Prayer of the Heart
in Syriac Tradition," *Sobornost* 4 (1982) 135-136.

[19]Bedjan, *Mar Isaacus,*, pp. 166-167.

probably due to the fact that few achieve this level and that, in any case, the way of the spiritual person is not perceptible to humans, not even to demons, but only to the Lord. Knowledge is the ladder by which one ascends to faith, but knowledge becomes dispensable once faith is reached. From this point on, the spiritual light of faith which shines in the soul by grace takes the place of knowledge. Some even say that, for Isaac, prayer is superseded.[20]

This final stage seems to coincide with the resurrected life, during brief moments of wonder, as a foretaste of the future aeon:

> And so from here one is easily moved towards what is called unified knowledge which is, according to a clear interpretation, wonder in God. This is the order of that great way which is to come which will be given in the freedom of immortal life, in that way of life which is after the resurrection.[21]

"Wonder" occurs in other East Syrian writers as well. John of Dalyatha says that "continual prayer is wonder before God."[22] In the literature it sometimes appears as an attitude of wonder and praise at the *mirabilia Dei*. In other cases, it is recorded as lasting "three hours," indicating perhaps something more basic to East Syrian

---

[20]See E. Khalifé-Hachem, "La prière pure et la prière spirituelle selon Isaac de Ninive," in *Mémorial Mgr Gabriel Khouri-Sarkis*, ed. by F. Graffin (Louvain: Imprimerie Orientaliste, 1969), pp. 157-172.

[21]Bedjan, *Mar Isaacus*, p. 304. This definition of "unique" or "unified" knowledge is attributed to Theodore of Mopsuestia by E. Khalifé-Hachem. See his article "Isaac de Ninive," *Dictionnaire de Spiritualité*, 1971, VII, 2049.

[22]See Robert Beulay, "Jean de Dalyatha," *Dictionnaire de Spiritualité*, 1974, VIII, 451.

phenomenology. But Isaac's sense of wonder cannot be understood apart from a Christian phenomenology of the mercy of God and of personal humiliation consciously desired and accepted. It is by a path of humiliation that one is led to ecstatic admiration and overflowing joy for the wonders of God. Finally, "wonder" has a cosmic dimension:

> Read the two Testaments which God has continued for the knowledge of the whole world, that by the power of his Divine Economy the [world] be provided with food in every generation and be enveloped in wonder.[23]

Glossary

Isaac's writings became popular in his own East Syrian Church shortly after his death. Quickly, Jacobites appreciated his sanctity and spiritual insight; and by changing a few names such as those of Theodore of Mopsuestia and Diodorus of Tarsus, they were able to consider him one of their own. Writers cited by Isaac include Basil, Athanasius, Ephrem, Pseudo-Dionysius, Theodore of Mopsuestia, Diodorus of Tarsus, Evagrius, Macarius, John of Apamea, and the Fathers of Scete. Isaac does not always identify his sources. Sometimes others have removed names from the text for polemical purposes; but the particle *lam* in the Syriac text always indicates the presence of a quote, simplifying to some degree the identification of sources. The following authors have either influenced Isaac, or they are part of the same East Syrian spirituality and, when considered together, they offer points of com-

---

[23]See Trans., 4th Disc., #57.

parison which help us to understand Isaac's writings in all their complexity.

The influence of Evagrius (+399) is very strong in Syriac spirituality. Though his writings were condemned by the Greeks in 553 because of his Origenistic tendency, most of them were retained in Syriac. Paradoxically, Monophysites and Nestorians agreed in their anti-Origenism, while Nestorians embraced the Origenistic Evagrius. Isaac quotes him many times by name and at other times anonymously. Evagrius shaped the basic concepts of ascetic vocabulary for all East Syrian writers, including St Isaac: *hesychia; praktike; logismoi* and classification of thoughts into eight groups; passions and *apatheia; gnosis; theoria.* The development of this vocabulary was a significant doctrinal addition to spirituality in general, and to the East Syrian tradition in particular. St Isaac is incomprehensible without a basic understanding of Evagrius.

Macarius, Pseudo-Macarius, or Symeon of Mesopotamia, was a monk who lived at the end of the fourth century. He is often confused with Macarius of Egypt, a celebrated fourth-century monk of Scete and collaborator of St Anthony. Pseudo-Macarius lived in Mesopotamia, near Asia Minor. His language is generally biblical and practical, monastic rather than philosophical. Certain tendencies, however, such as his understanding of the role of experience and human effort in the work of salvation, led to his being considered a Messalian.[24] The Macarian homilies, the writings of Ephrem, and the *Liber Graduum* are all influenced by this experiential tradition. Isaac too draws from it, as when he denies that spiritual knowledge can be gained by intellectual knowledge. Signs of grace

---

[24]See J. Meyendorff, "Messalianism or Antimessalianism? A Fresh Look at the Macarian Problem," in *Kiriakon,* Festschrift J. Quasten, t. 2 (Munster, 1970), pp. 585-590.

such as tears, and humility understood as the "garment of divinity" and the fruit of love, are ideas inspired by Macarius. One must not underestimate his importance in the discourses of Isaac.

John the Solitary wrote in the second half of the fifth century. There is confusion about his identity, and he is variously referred to as John of Lycopolis, John of Apamea and John the Solitary of Apamea. This confusion was possibly created in order to polemize his writings during the sixth-century Syrian doctrinal disputes. He seems to be West Syrian theologically, but he was read eagerly by East Syrians. As with Isaac, his spiritual greatness empowered him to transcend ecclesial boundaries. John the Solitary seems to be natively Syrian, with no trace of Evagrius or Pseudo-Dionysius, whereas the influence of Theodore of Mopsuestia on his cosmology is probable. But the basis for all his doctrine is Scripture. John himself says that what is essential is to return constantly to the "assiduous frequentation of the Word of light." Grounded in Scripture, his whole thought is dominated by hope in the world to come. This hope guides his understanding of the Divine Economy of salvation (*oikonomia*). It also guides his understanding of the nature of the individual spiritual life, that is, of the tripartite division (body—soul—spirit), which so influenced Isaac.

Abba Isaiah, author of an *Asceticon*, was long considered as an Egyptian monk of the fifth century. Recent scholarship, however, has maintained the hypothesis that he was from Gaza. The recent publication of the Syriac text of the *Asceticon*, translated *ca.* 550 from the Greek, points to the possibility of more than one author.[25] The *Asceticon* is closely connected to and has been generated

---

[25]See L. Regnault, "Isaie de Scété ou de Gaza," *Dictionnaire de Spiritualité*, 1971, VII:2, 2083-2095.

by apophthegmatic literature. Since formation of candidates to the anchoretic life was the scope of apophthegmatic literature, so also in the *Asceticon* the didactic or pedadogic dimension is strong. A rigorous asceticism pervades the work, and this may be what endeared it to the Syrians with their encratite tendencies.

Stephen Bar Sudaili was born in Edessa and lived as a monk in Jerusalem *ca.* 500. He is generally considered to be the author of the *Book of Hierotheos*.[26] This work has many apparent similarities to the writings of Isaac of Nineveh, though with a greater concentration on the higher states of mysticism than Isaac tends to express. Bar Sudaili is concerned with cosmology, with the ascent of the mind, and with the consummation of all things. Jewish apocalyptic, particularly millenaristic, influences have been noted in the work. Evagrius influenced his cosmology. In addition, aspects of Origen's mysticism, as mediated by Evagrius, can be found. Finally, the *Book of Hierotheos* also bears some resemblance to the Pseudo-Dionysian corpus.

Anan-Isho was born in Adiabene. With his brother he became a monk at Izla and, after a pilgrimage to Jerusalem, spent a prolonged period at Scete. When he returned from Egypt he entered the monastery of Bet Abhe. It is quite possible that he and Isaac were contemporaries there. Because he was a good musician, he was asked by the Catholicos to work on the *Hudra,* and because of the quality of this work, he was asked to arrange and translate the *Paradise* of Palladius for use by the Syrians, *ca.* 650. Palladius must already have been known in Persia before the edition of Anan-Isho, but this

---

[26]F. S. Marsh, *The Book of the Holy Hierotheos* (London: Williams and Norgate, 1927).

new edition became the standard for access to the world of the Fathers of Scete.[27]

Dadisho of Qatraya originated from along the Persian Gulf in the second half of the seventh century. Time and geography place him very close to Isaac of Nineveh. Dadisho's extant works consist of a *Discourse on Solitude* and a commentary on the *Asceticon* of Abba Isaiah.[28] From the *Asceticon* he discerned certain doctrinal principles and organized them into a system which characterizes the whole of his commentary. Dadisho's synthesis and vocabulary are not merely a reflection of the *Asceticon,* although the two are very close. Of particular interest for a better understanding of Isaac is the use of the term *theoria* by Dadisho: he understands it to be a work and manifestation of the Spirit. *Theoria* is a complex concept describing various valences, both hermeneutical and spiritual. Dadisho's other work, the *Discourse on Solitude,* is conveniently available in the Mingana collection. In this long treatise he describes the spiritual exercises of monks in Mesopotamia during their customary yearly, seven-week long retreat.

John of Dalyatha, an eighth-century Nestorian, is quite similar to Isaac. The fine edition of John's delightful letters by Robert Beulay in *Patrologia Orientalis* permits a verification and illumination by the comparison of some key concepts in Isaac. For example, John of Dalyatha continues the tripartite division of the mystical way, a notion he also inherits from John the Solitary. John of Dalyatha's writings may have undergone early Nestorian revision, since he was censured by Timothy at the East Syrian Synod in 786-787 because of Messalian tendencies.

---

[27]See E.A.W. Budge, *Stories of the Holy Fathers* (Oxford: University Press, 1934).

[28]R. Draguet, ed. and tr., *Commentaire du Livre d'Abba Isaie par Dadisho Qatraya,* CSCO, Syr. 150-151 (Louvain, 1973).

But his emphasis on the sacramental dimension of the mystic way as "anticipated resurrection," the fruit of Baptism and Eucharist, would seem to contradict the Messalian charge. There is also some Evagrian influence in his writings.

Joseph Hazzaya was an East Syrian monk of the eighth century, born in Nimrod, son of a Magian chief. He was sold into service for several years to a Muslim, then to a Christian. While serving the Christian family, he himself became a Christian, and his master freed him because of his great love of prayer. Joseph then became a monk in northern Iraq. He wrote a great deal, about 1,900 treatises; not all have survived.[29] The basic tripartite phenomenology of the mystical way characterizes his works as well. He was also accused of certain Messalian tendencies, but here again his insistence on the sacraments makes the legitimacy of the censure questionable. The principal accusation against him, however, was that he believed in the vision of the Divinity as part of the mystical way. For Nestorians, this vision was inadmissible even for the humanity of Christ. Joseph is considered to be the theoretician of East Syrian mysticism.

Though the emphasis here is on monastic authors, we would be remiss in not mentioning also an important theological distinction between two other authors who influenced Isaac, as well as the whole East Syrian tradition. Theodore of Mopsuestia criticizes the cosmology of Origen and offers instead a concept of the world more in conformity with Scripture.[30] Instead of two successive creations with a subsequent "fall," as described by Origen, Theodore presents a radically different view of two contiguous *katastaseis*, or "ages," both willed by God, not

---

[29]See R. Beulay, "Joseph Hazzaya," *Dictionnaire de Spiritualité*, 1974, VIII, 1341-1349.

[30]See Guillaumont, *'Kephalia Gnostica'*, pp. 183-186.

susceptible to "fall." Theodore's cosmology becomes of paramount importance in East Syrian exegetical and spiritual literature in the development of the concept of Divine Economy (*oikonomia*). This concept is found throughout the writings of Isaac.

In conclusion to this attempt to establish a glossary, it should be noted that only a tiny fraction of this information appears in the translation of Isaac by A. J. Wensinck.[31] This is unfortunate, for it makes Isaac inaccessible. Wensinck, because of his concerns for Islamic mysticism, has made very little effort to situate Isaac in his own tradition, whereas it is not possible to understand him apart from his tradition. "Tradition in the early Church was first of all a hermeneutical principle and method."[32] Scripture and patristic writings can be fully understood only in the context of the living tradition which is an integral dimension of Christian existence. Tradition does not add to the writings but provides the "living context, the comprehensive perspective," in which the design and intention of the writings can be understood."[33]

This translation has been made on the basis of the Syriac text edited by P. Bedjan in *Mar Isaacus Ninivita, De Perfectione Religiosa*, pp. 1-99.

[31]A. J. Wensinck, tr. *Mystic Treatises by Isaac of Nineveh* (Wiesbaden, 1969).

[32]See G. Florovsky, "The Function of Tradition in the Ancient Church," *Holy Cross Theological Review* IX, 2 (1963-64) 181-200.

[33]*Ibid.*

The translator particularly wishes to thank John Marks, Professor of Near Eastern Studies at Princeton University, for his encouragement and assistance in this translation. Thanks are also due to Prof. Sebastian Brock of Oxford University, Sr. Maria Gallo, translator of Isaac into Italian, and the Rev. Gerard Sloyan, Ph.D. of Temple University.

Nativity of the Mother of God
September, 1987

ADDITIONAL BIBLIOGRAPHY

BROCK, S.P. "St Isaac of Nineveh and Syriac Spirituality." *Sobornost* 7 (1975) 79-89.

FIEY, J. M. *Jalons pour une histoire de l'église en Iraq,* CSCO 310, 1970.

LABOURT, J. *Le Christianisme dans l'Empire Perse* (Paris, 1904).

MILLER, D. tr. *Ascetical Homilies of St Isaac of Nineveh* (Boston, 1984).

MURRAY, ROBERT. *Symbols of Church and Kingdom. A Study in Early Syriac Tradition* (London: Cambridge University Press, 1975).

SMITH, M. *Studies in Early Mysticism in the Near and Middle East* (London, 1931).

VOOBUS, A. *History of Asceticism in the Syrian Orient,* 2 vols. CSCO, Subsidia 17 (Louvain, 1958-60).

WALLACE-HADRILL, D. S. *Christian Antioch. A Study of Early Christian Thought in the East* (Cambridge: Cambridge University Press, 1982).

FIRST DISCOURSE

1. The beginning of virtue is the fear of God [which], is said [to be] the offspring of faith.[1] Indeed it is sown in the heart when a man allows his mind to contain its roving impulses from the distractions of the world within the inner illuminations which arise from reflection on the order of the things to come. In laying the foundation of virtue, the first of its peculiar elements is when we withdraw ourselves in flight from things toward the luminous word of the straight and holy paths,[2] that word which was called an enlightener by the Psalmist inspired by the Holy Spirit.[3]

2. It is difficult to find anyone who is able to bear honors, or it may be that there is no such person, on account of his ready capacity for change, even if, as one says, he is like an angel in his way [of life].[4]

3. The beginning of the way of life[5] consists in applying the mind to the words of God and in exercising patience. For the draught which comes from the words of God helps toward the perfection which is in the latter. Likewise, indeed, the increase of growth in the fulfillment of patience gives place to a greater need for the words of

---

[1]Cf. Evagrius, *Praktikos,* ch. 81.
[2]Ps 25:10.
[3]Ps 119:105.
[4]Ps 8:5.
[5]Ps 16:11.

God. And the help which is from both of them quickly brings about the elevation of the whole edifice.

4.   No one is able to draw near to God without leaving the world far behind. By leaving the world I do not mean departing from the body but rather leaving bodily affairs behind.

5.   This is virtue: emptying one's mind of the world. As long as the senses are occupied with things, the heart cannot stop imagining them. Passions do not cease nor evil thoughts come to an end without the desert and solitude.

6.   For until the soul is intoxicated with faith in God, thus receiving a sense of its powers, the weakness of the senses will not be healed and the soul cannot trample down visible matter, which is a screen against what is within and not perceived.

7.   Reason is the cause of freedom. The fruit of both is a tendency to deviate. Without the first the second cannot be. And where freedom is lacking, the tendency to deviate is bound as if with bridles.

8.   A person in whom grace abounds loves righteousness and so rejects the fear of death. The soul of such a person finds many reasons why one should endure afflictions because of the fear of God. Those things which are harmful for the body and which are reluctantly sustained by nature and consequently cause pain are considered as nothing when compared with what is awaited.[6] The person's mind is fully persuaded that no one can know truth without gaining experience of suffering; also that God provides very carefully for man, so that he is not abandoned to chance. Those especially who have gone out in search of Him and who have borne suffering for his sake see this clearly, in colors as it were. When, however, lack of faith is planted in our heart, all

---

[6]Cf. Rom 8:18.

of these things are experienced as contradictions and not for the sake of testing. The taunts that trust in God does not "pay off" and that God is not so concerned for you as He is thought to be, which are frequently buzzed by those who lie in wait and shoot their arrows from ambush— these taunts are not worthy of response.

9. The beginning of a person's true life is the fear of God.[7] But this fear does not consent to remain in the soul together with the distraction of things. For when the heart serves the senses it is distracted from the sweetness which is in God.

10. The inner impulses are bound in their perceptions by reason of the senses which serve them.

11. A divided heart makes the soul afraid, but faith can strengthen the mind even when the body is mutilated. As long as the love of the body is strong in you, you cannot be courageous and unafraid; for whatever is loved, constantly harbors many adversaries.

12. Anyone who is intent on honor will not lack occasions for grief.

13. There is no one whose mind, when outward circumstances change, does not receive correspondingly equal changes.

14. If there is indeed a second perception of the senses from which desire is naturally begotten, as Evagrius says,[8] then let them keep silent who think to keep the mind in peace in spite of anxieties.

15. This one is chaste: not only the one from whom are withheld hateful impulses at the time of conflict but the one whose steadfast heart chastens the gaze of his mind, lest it boldly fix its gaze on lascivious thoughts. And while the holiness of his mind will be attested to by the faithfully guarded gaze of his eyes, modesty will

---

[7] Cf. Prov 1:7.
[8] Evagrius, *Praktikos*, ch. 4.

be like a veil hung at the secret place of his thoughts. Thus his mind's purity, like that of a chaste virgin, is guarded faithfully for Christ.[9]

16. Nothing can so banish licentious habits from the soul and restrain memories which disturb and stir up troubling flames in the body as can avid devotion to the love of learning and searching investigation into the meanings of the passages of Scripture.

17. When the impulses of the soul plunge into the pleasure which comes from the wisdom stored in the words of Scripture, vigorously drawing understanding from it, a person will leave his body behind. Such a one will forget the world and all that is in it and will cancel from the soul all the memories which stir up images of the material world. Often the soul in wonder desists in its reflection from the use of habitual thoughts which come naturally to it, in the presence of the novelties which come to it from the sea of the Scriptures' mysteries.

18. Even if the mind is floating in its upper waters, not being able to make its impulses probe the whole depth of the sea to discern all the treasures which are in its depths, still meditation is able with its desire to bind firmly the thoughts of the mind with thoughts of wonder, hindering them from thinking and running after the natural body, as a man who is clothed in God has said.[10]

19. "Indeed because the heart is weak," he says, "it cannot bear the evils which reach it from without nor the struggle which is within." "And you know," he continues, "that the evil thought of the body is strong. And if the heart is not engaged in study, it is not able to bear the tumult of the body's thought."

20. For as the weight of the balance diminishes its rapid motion against the breeze, so modesty and fear

---

[9]2 Cor 11:2.
[10]Cf. Gal 3:27.

diminish the tendency of the mind to deviate. What is analogous to the decrease in the speed of the balance is the diminution of the mind's abundant power of freedom for deviation. In the case of the balance, the lighter its pans the greater freedom they have to move. Likewise, when the soul is freed because fear is lifted from it, the balance of the mind is suddenly lightened on every side. Thus, continual movement follows upon freedom, and inconstancy of mind follows the tendency to deviation.

21. Be wise and place the foundation of your journey in the way of God. In a few days it will bring you to the gate of the Kingdom without deviation.

22. For education in your way of life, do not look at the sentences laid down for examination—as those who are trained by teachers do—so that your soul is exalted by the importance of the considerations which are in them. Rather distinguish the meaning of the word in all the stories that you find in the Scriptures, that you may deepen your soul to dwell with the great insights which are in the statements of those who are illumined.

23. Those who are led by grace to illumination in their way of life constantly perceive an intelligible ray, as it were, which passes through the words of Scripture. The ray distinguishes before the mind ordinary speech from the discourses which are spoken with greatness of meaning for the illumination of the soul.

24. One who reads great works in an ordinary way also profanes his heart, depriving it of that holy power which gives it a sweet taste with meanings which fill the soul with wonder. All things run toward their likeness. And the soul in which there is a portion of the Spirit,[11] when it hears something with a spiritual power hidden in it, ardently draws out the story; although a story which

---

[11]Cf. Wis 12:1.

is told spiritually, with a great power hidden in it, does not excite everyone to admiration.

25. A word concerning virtue requires a heart emptied of earth and its affairs.

26. If a person's mind is wearied by solicitude for transitory things, discourses concerning virtue will not stir his thought to desire [virtue] ardently.

27. Liberation from material impulses precedes bonds in God, as it were by essence. And though, as if by divine providence of grace, sometimes the latter precedes the former so that love surpasses love,[12] still, in the usual order of the divine economy, common succession is different. You then observe the common order. If grace precedes you, it is for its own sake. If not, you must ascend the spiritual tower along the way everyone goes by tradition.

28. Everything which is done in contemplation and the commandment fulfilled because of it is wholly invisible to the eyes of the flesh. But everything which is done in practice is wholly complex. For it is a single commandment which requires both, that is, contemplation and practice; because corporeity and non-corporeity and the interaction of the two constitute the whole. For this reason and that which derives from it, the illumined intellect understands in a twofold way, both what is simple and mystical and what is composite, as was formerly commanded by means of the blessed Moses.[13]

29. Works which are done with great care by the pure do not remove the perception of culpable things

---

[12]Cf. Jn 1:16.

[13]Jewish traditions of exegesis, of which there are numerous examples in East Syrian Christian literature, see an intrinsic unity between Scripture and its interpretation and trace back to Sinai the reception both of the oral and the written Law. Many examples of this understanding can be found in most rabbinical collections, such as *Midrash Rabbah*.

done previously, but the sting of its memory is taken from the mind, so that even its passage in the mind becomes useful.

30. The insatiable longing of the soul for the acquisition of virtue surpasses the desire of its partner, the body, for visible things.

31. Measure adorns everything. For without it even those things which are perceived as helpful will turn their use to harm without any hindrance at all.

32. Do you desire to have communion with God in your mind by receiving the perception of that delight which is not subject to the senses? Cleave to mercy. For if [mercy] is found within you, it is formed by that holy beauty which it resembles. All acts of mercy will make the soul a partaker without delay, in the unique glory of the divine rank.

33. Spiritual union is a watchful memory which without division swells the heart with burning compassion. That union has its bond strengthened by constancy in the commandments; and neither figuratively nor in a natural way is matter found here for the vision of the soul on which it may rely hypostatically. Thus, the heart is drawn to wonder by the closing of its two senses, the physical and the spiritual. There is no other way to spiritual love, which forms the invisible image, than before all else to begin with mercy according to the word of our Lord who, with respect to the perfection of the Father, the foundation, lays this command on those who obey Him.[14]

34. A word of action is different from beautiful words. Even without the test of experience, wisdom knows how to adorn its words and to speak the truth without acquaintance with it and to expatiate on virtue without ever having borne the experience of putting it into practice. A word derived from practice is a treasure of trust.

---

[14]Cf. Mt 5:48; Lk 6:36.

Idle wisdom, however, is a deposit of shame, as when an artist who paints water on walls cannot quench his thirst by it, and as one who sees beautiful dreams.

35. But one who speaks about virtue from the experience of his own labor brings a word to his hearers, as it were, from the riches of his commerce. And he sows his doctrine in the ears of his listeners as from the goods of his soul. He opens his mouth with confidence before his spiritual sons in the manner of aged Jacob to chaste Joseph. "Behold I have given you one portion more than to your brothers which I took from the hand of the Amorites with my sword and with my bow."[15]

36. Everyone, then, whose way of life is sullied will cherish this life, as will the one who is lacking in knowledge. Someone has said rightly, "The fear of death distresses the man of flesh, but the one who has a good witness in his soul earnestly desires death as he does life."

37. Do not reckon as truly wise anyone whose mind is subjected to fear because of this life.

38. Reckon as dreams all the good and evil things which happen to the body. Not only will you be liberated from them by death, but often even before death they will leave you and disappear.

39. But if your soul is a partaker in some of them, consider them as your possession forever, even as going with you to the future world. If they are beautiful rejoice and thank God in your mind. But if they are evil be sorrowful and lament and seek deliverance from them while you are in the body. As for all the good which is done to you mystically and in secret, you will be sure that baptism and faith are its mediators to you, by which you were called to good works in Jesus Christ. To Him and to his Father and to the Holy Spirit be praise and honor and adoration now and always and forever and ever. Amen.

---

[15]Gen 48:22.

SECOND DISCOURSE

1. The gratitude of the recipient stimulates the donor to gifts greater than before. One who defrauds in little things is also deceitful and unjust in greater things.[16]

2. The sick one who is familiar with his illness is easily cured and the one who acknowledges his pain is close to healing.[17]

3. The pains of a hard heart grow in number and the sick person who resists the physician increases his own suffering.

4. There is no sin without forgiveness except that one which is without repentance. And there is no gift which is without increase except the one which lacks acknowledgement. For the fool's portion is small in his eyes.

5. Be mindful always of those who are superior to you in virtue that you may see yourself at all times as being less in comparison with them. And consider at all times the mighty afflictions of those whose anxieties are grievous and cruel so that you may be grateful for the lesser things which happen to you and be able to bear them with joy.

6. When you are defeated, depressed and slothful; bound and ensnared before your adversary by terrible

---

[16]Cf. Sir 19:1; Lk 16:10.
[17]1 Jn 1:8-9.

misery and by weariness from the practice of sin, bring to your mind the former times of diligence and how even in little things you showed care and were moved with zeal against those who would impede your course. You sighed for the sake of the little things which you neglected accidentally and you were utterly weaving a crown of victory with them. Then by these and similar memories your soul will be aroused as from the depth and be clad with a blaze of zeal. And as from the dead it will arise from its torpor and rise up and come to its former state in the heated struggle against Satan and sin.[18]

7. Remember the fall of the strong that you may be humble in your virtues. Call to mind the severity of the sins of those who fell and repented as well as the exaltation and honor which they received afterward, so that you may be encouraged in your repentance.

8. Persecute yourself and your adversary will be driven away from you.

9. Be at peace with your soul and heaven and earth will be at peace with you. Endeavor to enter the treasury within you and you will see that treasury which is in heaven. The former and the latter are one and through a single entrance you will see both of them. The ladder of that kingdom is hidden within you, within your soul. Dive away from sin into yourself and there you will find the steps by which you may ascend.

10. The Scriptures have not explained what are the things of the future world. But they have taught us plainly how we might receive even now the perception of their delight without change of nature or shift of place.

11. And even if, as an incentive to us, they have given them beloved names of glorious things, which are agreeable and precious to us, still, by saying that eye has not seen

---

[18]Cf. Is 59:17; Wis 5:16f.; Eph 6:14f.; 1 Thess 5:6f., etc.

nor ear heard, and so on,[19] [the Scriptures] make known to us that those future things in their incomprehensibility are in no way similar to anything in this life. It is a question of spiritual delight which is not the quality of the things themselves but it is announced to us that those who enjoy it are already found in the future world. Otherwise it would not be written: "the kingdom of God is within you"[20] and "Thy kingdom come."[21] Therefore we possess in us a fullness of perceptible things as pledge[22] of the delight that is in them. Indeed it is necessary that there be a resemblance between these and the pledge, partial now, but in complete perfection in the world to come.[23] Also that the word "as in a mirror"[24] in every way shows the possession of a resemblance, not the possession of a reality. Now if according to the trustworthy witnesses of the commentators of the Scriptures, this is the effect of an intelligible operation of the Holy Spirit, also this is part of that totality. Then, apart from the spiritual operation that in the intelligible perception mediates between the Spirit and those on which it operates, the delight of the saints does not have any sensible intermediary, neither of the senses nor of sensible objects there, other than the vessels,[25] that in a certain way contain all that delight. We may say that it concerns an effusion of light but not intelligible light.

12. The friend of virtue is not the one who diligently does beautiful things, but the one who gladly accepts the evil things which cling to him.

13. That one endure misfortunes for the sake of

---

[19]1 Cor 2:9.
[20]Lk 17:21.
[21]Mt 6:10.
[22]2 Cor 1:22.
[23]1 Cor 13:9-10.
[24]1 Cor 13:12.
[25]Cf. Acts 9:15.

virtue is not as great as that in the persuasion of entice-
ments, the mind not be disturbed precisely because of the
choice of one's good will.

14. For any repentance which follows the removal of
freedom cannot be a source of joy nor reckoned as a
reward of those who repent.

15. Cover the sinner even though you are not harmed
by him. Indeed, encourage him for life and the mercy of
the Lord will sustain you.

16. Support the weak and distressed with a word as
far as you are able, that the right hand upholding the
universe may sustain you.

17. Be a companion to those who are sad at heart
with passionate prayer and heartfelt sighs; then a fountain
of grace will be opened before your petitions. Weary
yourself in petition at all times before God,[26] with a heart
bearing pure thoughts filled with contrition, and He will
guard your mind from impure thoughts so that the way
of God not be made contemptible in you. Saturate your
gaze with constant study of the lections of Scripture, so
that idleness will not be the occasion for an unusual vision
to be sullied in your sight.

18. Do not tempt your mind, for the sake of experience, by looking at base, seductive thoughts, while
supposing that you are invincible. Even wise men have
been troubled in this situation and gone wrong. Do not
take fire into your bosom as has been said.[27] Without
severe afflictions of the body it is difficult for the untrained
youth to be bound under the yoke of holiness.[28]

19. The sign in the soul which reveals the onset of
thick darkness of mind is this: negligence, at first in the
divine office and in prayer. For unless you fall from

---

[26]Cf. 1 Thess 5:17.
[27]Cf. Prov 6:27.
[28]Cf. Sir 7:23; 30:1-13.

there in the first place, a path of error cannot be opened in your soul. Then when you are deprived of God's help, which serves as a way to Him, you will fall readily into the hands of the adversary. And further! When you have no care for the things of virtue, then you will be carried off by all means to those things which are contrary. Any departure from one side is the beginning of an approach to the opposite side. Let the work of virtue prevail in your soul; reflect on it, et cetera.

20. Manifest your weakness before God at all times, lest strangers test your strength while you are separated from your helper.

21. The work of the cross is twofold. And this corresponds to the duality of nature which is divided into two parts: into endurance of bodily afflictions which comes about through the energy of the irascible part of the soul and is called practice; and into the subtle work of the mind in sacred studies and constant prayer and so forth, which is done with that desiring part and is called contemplation. Practice purifies the passionate part through the power of zeal; contemplation refines that part capable of knowing by means of the energy of the love of the soul, which is its natural longing.

22. Therefore whoever before discipline in the former part passes eagerly—not to say slothfully—to that second because of its sweetness, brings to pass the anger which God breathes against him. This is because before he has put to death his members that are on the earth,[29] namely, before he has healed the sickness of his thoughts by patiently enduring the labor and shame of the cross, he has presumed to imagine in his mind the glory of the cross. And this is what was said by the saints of old: "If the mind desires to ascend the cross before the senses

---

[29]Col 3:5.

cease from weakness, the anger of God will attack it."[30]

23.   The ascent of the cross that brings wrath is not the first part, that is the endurance of afflictions which is called crucifixion of the body; but the ascent of contemplation which is the second part, that which follows the healing of the soul. Indeed, the one who, while his mind is defiled with shameful passions, hastens to imagine in his heart illusory ideas about the future, will be silenced with punishment. This is because, without first purifying his mind by means of the afflictions incurred in subjugating the desires of the flesh,[31] he ran headlong, on the basis of what he had heard and read, to travel a path full of darkness, being blind. Even those whose sight is sound and full of light and who have grace as a guide are in peril, night and day. With eyes full of tears they continue in prayer and weeping night until day, for fear of the journey and the arduous precipices they happen upon, and the appearances of truth which are frequently found among its imitators on the path. For the things of God come of their own accord when you are not aware of them, if the place of your heart is pure and undefiled. If the small pupil of your soul has not been purified do not presume to gaze at the sphere of the sun lest you be deprived altogether of sight (which is sincere faith and humility and heartfelt confession and a little work according to your strength) and you be cast into one of the immaterial places which is darkness without God, like that one who presumed to enter the banquet in dirty clothes.[32]

24.   From labor and vigilance flows purity of thoughts; and from purity of thoughts the light of conscience. And

---

[30]See Abba Isaiah, Logos 17 Gr./26.4 Syr.; Hervé de Broc, tr., *Recueil Ascétique,* Spiritualité Orientale Vol. VII (Maine et Loire: Abbaye de Bellefontaine, 1976), p. 149.

[31]Gal 5:16.

[32]Cf. Mt 22:2-14.

from here the mind is guided by grace towards that which the senses have no power to teach or to learn.

25. Think of virtue as being the body, but of contemplation as being the soul; and of the two as being one complete spiritual person, composed of sensible and intelligible parts. Now, just as it is impossible for the soul to come into existence and birth without the complete formation of the body, so it is impossible that contemplation which is the second soul, the spirit of revelations, be formed in the womb of the intellect, capable of receiving an abundance of spiritual seed, without the bodily practice of virtue, where the knowledge that can receive revelations dwells.

26. Contemplation (*theoria*) is the perception of the divine mysteries hidden in the things which are spoken [in the Scriptures].

27. When you hear about renunciation of the world or about abandonment of the world or about being pure of the world, first of all you need to learn and know, not approximately but with powers of discernment: what the term, world, means and of how many distinctions this term consists. Only then will you be able to know your soul, how much you are distant from or connected to the world. If one first does not know what the world is, one will not understand with how many parts of the body one is distant or ensnared within it.

28. Many of those who withhold themselves from the world in two or three respects think that their souls are particularly separated from it by their way of life. This is because they have not understood or perceived wisely that in one or two parts they are dead to the world, while in all other parts they are alive within the body of the world. Therefore they are not even able to perceive their passions; and, because they do not perceive them, they are not even concerned about their healings.

29. According to contemplative inquiry, world is said

to be a general word which refers to distinct passions. When we want to speak of passions in general we call them "world." But when we speak of particular passions, we use their distinctive names.

30. The passions are part of the ongoing course of the world; and where the passions have ceased there the world has ceased proceeding on its course. The passions are: love of riches; amassing of possessions; the fattening of the body, from which proceeds carnal desire; love of honors, which is the source of envy; administration of government; pride and pomp of power; elegance; popularity, which is the cause of ill-will; fear for the body.

31. When these passions desist from their course, then correlatively the world ceases to exist. As in each of the saints who while living are dead, they are alive in the body but they do not live according to the flesh.[33] See in which of these you are alive and then you will know to what degree you are alive to the world and how much you are dead to it.

32. When you have learned what the world is, you will learn about these distinctions and also about your wallowing in it or being free of it.

33. In short, the world is the carnal way of life and the mind of the flesh. Further evidence for this is that negation of the world becomes apparent in these two changes: by a transformation in way of life and by a difference in mental impulses.

34. You may take the measure of your way of life by observing your mental impulses and the things towards which your mind wanders with its impulses: namely, for which things nature longs willingly, both those impulses that are habitual and those that are set in motion by chance; whether the mind receives the perception of incorporeal impulses only, or moves wholly through matter;

---

[33]Cf. Col 3:3; Rom 8:4.

whether this materiality is passional or a question of the imprints of corporeal practice [of virtue], in that the mind, not of its own will, is confused by those things with which it exercises virtue and from which it, not feebly, receives cause of fervor and concentration of thoughts, so that the mind [for its own education is still able][34] to labor bodily, with the right intention, although not passibly; and finally whether the mind is not distressed by the hidden attacks of the imprints of thoughts because of its excessive radiance in God which keeps cutting off vain memories. These brief indications of this chapter are sufficient for man's illumination, instead of many writings, if he is quiet and discerning.

35.   Fear for the body is strong in man so that many times he abstains from praiseworthy and honorable things because of it. But when fear for the soul beholds this, thus fear for the body is vanquished before it like wax by the force of the flame.[35]

---

[34]This is a variant from *Vatican Syr. 562*,f 6vb, 11.9-10, not used by Bedjan and which corrects his edition.
[35]Cf. Ps 68:2.

THIRD DISCOURSE

1. Any soul into whose nature there is no entry for increased anxiety about amassing goods does not require great care to find by and in itself impulses of wisdom about God. For that stillness of the soul from the world naturally arouses a slight stirring of thoughts in the soul, that by them it may be lifted to God and remain in wonder.

2. For when outside waters do not enter into the fountain of the soul, its natural waters spring up— wondrous thoughts they are, which are being continually moved toward God.

3. Whenever, then, the soul is found outside of this state, either the cause has proceeded from unusual recollections or the senses have stirred up commotion in the soul by concourse with things. But when the senses are shut in by unyielding stillness and memories grow dim with the help of this stillness, then you will see what is the nature of the thoughts of the soul, and what is the nature of the soul, and what treasures are stored in it. For the treasures are incorporeal intelligences which move of themselves without care or labor. For no man even knows how such thoughts are stirred up in human nature, nor who has been his teacher, nor how he has found that which—even when known—he does not know how to tell his companion, nor who was his spiritual guide towards that which he did not learn from another. This

is the nature of the soul. Therefore the passions are introduced to the soul by some cause. For by nature the soul is not subject to passion.

4. When you find natural and bodily passions mentioned in the Scriptures, corresponding causes are mentioned. The soul, however, does not naturally have passions.

5. But the philosophers who are outside do not believe this. Similarly neither do those who follow their thinking. We believe that God has not made his image subject to passion. For by his image I do not mean the body but the soul, that is, what is invisible. Now every image contains the likeness of an original. And a visible image cannot depict the likeness of something invisible. Therefore we believe that the passions of the soul are not natural as the philosophers maintain. If there is anyone who disputes this we will ask him to tell us, "What is natural to the soul? That it should be without passions while being filled with light, or that it should be agitated by the passions while in darkness?" Now if the nature of the soul is sometimes a limpid receptacle of the blessed light, it will also be found in this state when it comes again to its original created condition. But when it is moved by passions, all the members of the Church acknowledge that it has gone outside its nature. Therefore the passions [must have] entered the nature of the soul afterward; it is not right at all to consider passions to be natural to the soul. Even though the soul is moved by them, it is evident that it is moved by something outside of itself and not on its own. If these passions are considered natural to the soul because by them it is moved for the body's sake, then hunger and thirst and sleep belong to the soul too, because through them the soul together with the body suffers and is refreshed. Likewise the amputation of limbs and fever and pains and diseases etc., would belong to the soul, because the body suffers

from them through its participation with the soul, and the soul is moved with joy by the things of the body, suffering harm from the adversities of the body.

6. The nature of the soul: what is external to its nature, and what is above its nature. Natural to the soul is the understanding of all created things, perceptible and intelligible. Above its nature is its impulse from divine contemplation. External to its nature is its being moved by passions. Indeed, the victorious Basil, light of the world, speaks in this way: When the soul is in its natural state it is found above; but when it is not in its nature it is found beneath and on the earth. Therefore there are no passions above where the special place of the soul is said to be. But when nature descends from its order, then it becomes passible. Where, then, are the natural passions now that it is shown that they are not of the soul's nature? In this way, the soul is moved by the reprehensible passions of the body, as also it is moved by hunger and thirst because of the body. But since no laws have been laid down concerning these things, the soul is not guilty. Such also is sometimes the case when a person is commanded by God to do things which are blameworthy, but receives a reward instead of blame and censure, as with Hosea the prophet[36] who was made a partner in an unlawful marriage, and Elijah[37] who committed murder in his zeal for God, and those who at Moses' command stabbed their kinsmen with swords.[38] But besides these natural things of the body it is also said that anger and rage belong naturally to the soul, and that these are its passions.[39]

7. Second question. We ask further: when is the

---

[36]Cf. Hos 1:2.
[37]Cf. 1 Kgs 18:40.
[38]Cf. Ex 32:27.
[39]Cf. Evagrius, *Praktikos,* ch. 35.

desire of the soul natural? When it is inflamed by divine
things or indeed by those things of the earth and the
body? And when it is said that the soul's nature is inflamed by anger for those things, is this anger natural?
When is it *because of* the desire of the body, emulation,
praise, etc., and when is it *against* these? Let whoever con-
tends answer these questions for us and we will follow
up. For Holy Scripture says many things allegorically
and often it uses metaphors.

Often that which is of the body, Scripture imputes to
the soul. The things of the soul it likewise imputes to
the body without distinguishing them, so as not to prolong
the discourse. But the intelligent understand what they
read, that is, the sense of Scripture. For example Scripture attributes what is of the divinity of our Lord to his
excellent and sublime humanity, which is not compatible
with human nature or with his divinity. Many who do
not understand the language of Scripture have stumbled
here, falling without rising again. Thus it is also for the
things concerning the soul and the body. If virtue is the
natural health of the soul and the passions are diseases
which customarily befall nature and deprive it of its
health, it is evident that in nature health comes before
eventual illness. But if this is so, as indeed it is, then
virtue necessarily is connatural to the soul and the accidental is external to its nature because it is not possible
that what is first be not indeed natural.

8. Third question. Are bodily passions placed in the
body naturally or in a secondary way? And, as to the
soul, are the passions that affect it because of the body
secondary or natural? It is impossible to say that these
[passions] of the body are outside of nature. But of the
soul, because it is known and confessed by all to be
naturally pure, no one will venture to say of it that its
passibility is not metaphorical. For illness is acknowledged
as secondary to health and it is not possible that the

same thing be a good nature and an evil one. One of them necessarily precedes the other; and the one which precedes is natural. Whatever is accidental cannot be said to be natural or familiar but happens externally. Every chance and contingency, when it occurs, is joined to change and variation. But nature does not change nor does it vary. All existing passions are given for the support of each of the natures to which they belong naturally and for whose growth they were given by God. The bodily passions are placed in the body by God for its support and growth; the passions of the soul, that is, the soul's powers [are placed there] for the growth and support of the soul. When the body is constrained to go out from its passibility by abstaining from the passions in favor of the soul it is injured. Likewise, when the soul leaves what is its own and cleaves to that which is of the body it is injured. That is because, according to the word of the Apostle, "the spirit desires that which harms the body and the body desires that which harms the spirit. And the two of them are adversaries by nature."[40]

Therefore let no one blaspheme against God saying that He has placed passions and sin in our nature.[41] For in each of the natures which He fashioned, He placed something for its growth. But when one nature is joined to the other it is not found in what is proper to it but in what is not its own. And if these passions are naturally of the soul why then is it injured when it deals with them? For that which is peculiar to a nature does not harm it. And why is the complement of bodily passions for the growth and strength of the body, while those of the soul injure the soul if they are proper to it? And why does virtue torture the body but fatten the soul? You see how what is external to nature harms each of

[40]Gal 5:17.
[41]Cf. Js 1:13.

these natures. For each one of the natures rejoices when
it is near to what is proper to it. Do you want to know
what things are peculiar to each one of these natures?
Consider the things from whose use each one of the
natures draws profit: these are its own. If it is tormented
by these things, know that it is in the midst of what
is not its own.

In conclusion: if it is known that the passions of each
of these natures are opposites one to another, then everything which assists and gives rest to the body when the
soul uses it should not be considered to be of the soul's
nature, because these things which are of the soul's nature
are death to the body, except what is applied to the
soul in a metaphorical way. For as long as the soul is
clothed with the flesh, it cannot be freed completely
from the passions on account of the infirmity of the
flesh because of the union of its impulses with carnal
senses to which they are entwined with unsearchable
wisdom. Yet, though thus intermingled, the impulses of
the soul are distinct from the impulses of the body, and
the will of the soul is distinct from the will of the body,
in other words, flesh from spirit. Nature is utterly im-
perturbable and does not deny its properties. But, although a man brings each of the impulses to a greater
equality, in sin or in virtue, occasionally each of them
will move its will and pulsate according to its properties.
But when concern for the body is partially removed, its
impulses begin to move wholly in the Spirit, swimming
in the heart of heaven with incomprehensible things.
But the body does not cease from remembering what is
its own. And so even when the body's impulses are turned
to sin, the good things of the soul are not stilled by the
pulsation that is in the mind.

9. Of what does purity of mind consist? The "pure
of mind" is not a person who does not know evil things,
surely such a one would be an animal. Nor do we call

"pure of mind" those whom nature has placed in a condition of innocence,[42] unless we require that persons do not even belong to the order of created beings.[43] But purity of mind is captivation by divine things which comes about after the practice of many virtues.

10. We do not presume to say that one obtains [purity of mind] without the experience of opposing thoughts—otherwise he would not even be clothed with a body. For we cannot get rid of the contradictions of nature before the future world [is here]. By experience of thoughts, I do not mean that one should follow them, but rather it is the beginning of the struggle of thoughts which is provoked in the mind by the usual fourfold causes which put in motion all kinds of passions—so that in this life no one may be found who is above the memories of this life, even if he be one of the chiefs of the struggle who is considered to be perfect such as Paul.[44] But when the body by means of its impulses according to the natural order; and the world by means of its natures, in ministering to the senses; and the soul by means of thoughts and memories and powers of deviation; and demons by means of the disturbances of those things previously mentioned—though man is somewhat troubled by these four plagues which the passions inflict on him, he will be forcibly drawn to virtuous matters which are discerned by intellectual considerations. You judge whether one of these four things (body—world—soul—demons) can cease before the end of the world rather than by means of the transformation which death achieves. Judge if the body may be raised completely above its needs without nature constraining it to desire any of the things of this life. But if this is con-

---

42Cf. Mt 19:12.
43Job 4:17-18; 15:14-16.
44Cf. Rom 7:23.

sidered absurd, as long as these four plagues exist, the movement of the passions is necessary in every being clothed with a body, and vigilance is required of all. For I do not mean one or two of the passions but the whole variety of passions in those who are clothed with flesh. If someone were to presume that weakness of impulse means paucity of struggle, we would say to that one, whoever he be, that more labors are not needed but greater vigilance.

11. Of what does the difference between purity of mind and purity of heart consist? Purity of mind is different from purity of heart, just as there is a difference between a member of the body and the whole body. The mind is indeed one of the senses of the soul. But the heart is the ruler of the internal senses; that is, the sense of senses, which is the root. If the root is holy, so also are all the branches.[45] But the root is not holy even if in one of the branches there is holiness. The mind indeed with a little study of the Scriptures and a little labor in fasting and stillness forgets its former musing and is made pure, in that it becomes free from alien habits. It is also easily defiled. The heart, however, is purified with great sufferings and by being deprived of all mingling with the world, together with complete mortification in everything. When it has been purified, however, its purity is not defiled by contact with inconsequential things. That is, it is not afraid of violent battles, for it has a strong stomach which easily digests all foods hard for others who are ill in their abdomens. Physicians say that every kind of meat which is hard to digest gives greater strength to a healthy body when a strong stomach receives it. In the same way, every purification which is achieved easily, quickly and with little labor is easily defiled. But the purity acquired with great troubles over

---

[45]Rom 11:16, Peshitta.

a long period and by the highest part of the soul does not fear insignificant contacts with worldly things.

12. Chaste senses generate peace in the soul because they do not allow it to experience conflict. Indeed, unless [the soul] receives the sensation of something, that peace is a victory without struggle. But if [the soul] becomes negligent it will not know how to remain steadfast; and once a perception has entered, [the soul] must strive to repel the perception, destroying the previous qualities which are its natural limpidity and innocence. For most people, even perhaps all the world, for this reason depart from that first state. Only one out of many can be found who has returned to that first state by way of the second. Indeed innocence is much better than various kinds of forgiveness.

13. Fear is useful to human nature to preserve the boundary of transgressing a commandment.[46] But love is necessary to arouse in human nature a longing for good things, for the sake of which a person takes pains to do good works.

14. Spiritual knowledge is a consequence of the practice of good works. Both are preceded by love and fear. And fear precedes love. But everyone who presumes to acquire the latter things before the former surely lays the foundation for the ruin of his soul. God has set them in that order so that spiritual knowledge and love are begotten by fear and good works. Do not exchange the love of your neighbor for the love of things because that which is more precious than all things lies hidden within it.

15. That very thing which is a corporeal sign for the eyes of the flesh necessarily affects the secret gaze

---

[46]This reflects Rabbinic Judaism: "Make a fence around the Law," to protect the Law by surrounding it with cautionary rules. *Pirke Aboth* 1:1.

[of the soul]; moreover, the order of passions which causes the thick darkness for the soul's second natural contemplation does the same to natural stability;[47] and one is correlative to the other until the course of contemplations ceases.

16.   When the intellect is in a state of natural integrity it is in contemplation like that of the angels,[48] which is the first and natural contemplation,[49] and it is also called naked reason.[50] But when reason is in the second, natural knowledge, it sucks from material breasts and is nourished by the milk. This is called the last garment of the order previously mentioned; it is placed after purity in which the intellect enters first, that purity which is prior in existence, for it is the first degree of knowledge. But in honor it is last. And because of this it is called the secondary one according to some indications of the signs by which the intellect is purified and instructed for the ascent to the second degree, the perfection of the intellectual impulses and the degree which is near to divine contemplation.

17.   The senses are the last garment of the intellect.

---

[47]"Thick darkness," Ex 20.21 and Pseudo-Dionysius, *Mystical Theology*, ch. 1.

[48]According to East Syrian tradition, angels do not enjoy the vision of God.

[49]In the Evagrian schema of *theoria* there are two stages according to whether the object is God or created natures. The contemplation of created natures divides again between "second natural contemplation" and "first natural contemplation," depending on whether it has as its object visible or invisible natures. The contemplation of visible natures can already be spiritual according to Evagrius, for one goes beyond appearances to know the *logoi* which are part of the universe created by the Word of God. But in "first natural contemplation," the Christian actually becomes part of the other reality and understands as the angels do.

[50]"Naked reason" refers to immaterial contemplation occurring in the context of "first contemplation." The image is Evagrian. Through prayer the soul is restored to its function as mind (*nous*).

Its nakedness consists in its being moved by non-material contemplations.

18. Leave the things of no value that you may find precious things.

19. Be dead in life and you will not live in death. Let your soul die strenuously and not live in weakness. Not only those who, for the sake of faith in Christ suffer death, are martyrs; but also those who die because of their observance of his commandments.

20. Do not be foolish in your petitions lest you dishonor God by your ignorance.

21. Pray wisely that you may be deemed worthy of glorious things.

22. Seek precious things from the One who does not withhold; you will receive honor from Him because of the wise choice of your will.

23. Solomon asked for wisdom and he received an earthly kingdom with it because he knew how to ask wisely, that is, great things from the King.[51]

24. Elisha asked for a double share of his master's spirit and his request was not denied him.[52]

25. The King's honor is diminished by one who asks him for base things.

26. Israel sought contemptible things and received the wrath of God.

27. [Israel] neglected to marvel at [God's] deeds and his formidable works and sought the desires of her own belly. And while [the people's] food was in their mouths, God's anger arose upon [them].[53] Present your petitions to God according to his glory that your honor may be great before Him and He may rejoice in you.

28. As one who asks a full measure of dung from a

---

[51]Cf. 1 Kgs 3:4ff.
[52]Cf. 2 Kgs 2:9.
[53]Ps 78:30-31, Peshitta.

mighty king will not only be despised because of the
contemptibility of his petition which reveals his ignorance,
but also he insults the king with his foolish petition. Such
is the one who asks carnal things of God in prayer.

29. Behold the angels and the archangels, who are
the King's chiefs, look on you at the time of prayer to
see what petition you will present to their Lord. They
marvel at you when they see a carnal one abandon his
dunghill and ask for heavenly things.

30. Do not ask God for anything that even without
our request He takes care to give us. He does not withhold these things from his housemates,[54] nor from those
who are utterly alien to the knowledge of Him and who
do not even know that He exists.

31. "Do not be a prater like the heathens." What is
this "like the heathens"?[55] The peoples of the earth seek
these things of the body. But you do not think, "What
will we eat or what will we drink or with what will we
be clothed"? Your Father knows that these things are
necessary to you, too.[56]

32. A son never asks for bread from his father but
he presents petitions concerning the great portions which
will be his in his father's house.

33. That which our Lord commanded concerning
daily bread, namely to ask for it in prayer, is a petition
which He handed down to mankind in general because
of the weakness of its mind. But see what He commands
those who are perfect in knowledge and healthy in soul:
"Take no thought about food or clothing. If God cares
for birds which have no soul, how much more for you.
But seek from God the kingdom and righteousness and

---

[54]Cf. Heb 3:6; see also Macarian Homilies 49:4 (tr. A. J.
Mason).
[55]Mt 6:7.
[56]Mt 6:31f.

these things He will give to you over and above."[57]

34.   If He delays over your request, in that you seek but you do not readily receive, do not be grieved; for you are not wiser than God. When you wait like this it is either because your way of life does not conform with your request or because the ways of your heart differ from the purpose of your prayer; or because your inner state is like that of a child in comparison with the greatness of the matter.

35.   It is not fitting that great things fall readily into our hands, lest the gift of God be undervalued because of the ease of its discovery.

36.   Everything which is readily found is also easily lost.

37.   Everything which is gained with labor is guarded with vigilance.

38.   Thirst for Jesus, that He may intoxicate you with his love. Close your eyes to the precious things of the world that you may deserve to have the peace of God reign in your heart.

39.   Abstain from the attractions which glitter before the eyes, that you may be worthy of joy in the Spirit.

40.   If your way of life is not worthy of God do not ask Him for glorious things, that you may not appear as one who tempts God.

41.   Indeed, prayer corresponds directly with way of life.

42.   No one earnestly desires heavenly things while bound by voluntary bonds because of the body; and no one asks for these things while occupied with earthly things. The desire of everyone is known by his works; the things he cares about solicitously, he will ask for in prayer. And the things he prays for he will diligently demonstrate with deeds.

---

[57]Mt 6:25-26, 33.

43. Whoever desires great things is not engrossed with the lesser.

44. Be free while you are bound by the body and show submission in your freedom because of Christ; and be wise in your innocence lest you be seduced.

45. Love humility in your conduct that you may be delivered from the imperceptible snares which are always found beside the paths where the humble walk. Do not refuse tribulations, for by their means you will enter into knowledge.

46. Do not fear temptations, for in them you will find precious things.

47. Pray lest you enter into temptations of the soul. But for those of the body, make ready with all your strength and swim in them with every limb and muscle. Indeed apart from them it is not possible for you to draw near to God, for within them lies divine rest.

48. Whoever flees from temptation—not from temptations of desires but from tribulations—flees from virtue.

49. How does that saying, "Pray, lest you enter into temptation,"[58] compare to that other, "Strive to enter by the narrow gate,"[59] and, "Do not fear those who kill the body"[60] and, "Whoever loses his life for my sake will find it?"[61] In all these passages our Lord exhorts us concerning temptations. But in the first He commands us to pray lest we enter into temptation. What virtue is accomplished without temptations? Or what temptation is more serious than the loss which He commands us to undergo for his sake? "He who does not take up his cross and follow me is not worthy of me,"[62] and "Pray lest you enter into temptation"; but throughout his teach-

[58]Mt 26:41.
[59]Lk 13:24.
[60]Mt 10:28.
[61]Mt 10:39.
[62]Mt 10.38.

ing is scattered the entrance into temptations. For He has said: "Without temptations the kingdom of heaven will not be found."[63]

50. Oh how narrow is the way of your teaching, our Lord! And the one who does not discern with knowledge when he reads will always be outside it in his understanding.

51. When the sons of Zebedee and their mother besought Him for a seat with Him in the kingdom, He required this of them: would they be able to receive the cup of temptations gladly? "Are you able to drink the cup which I drink and to be baptized with the baptism that I am baptized with?"[64] And how is it, our Lord, that here you command: "Pray lest you enter into temptation"?

ABOUT WHICH TEMPTATIONS MUST WE PRAY NOT TO ENTER?

52. Pray that you do not enter into temptation about your faith.

53. Pray that through your mind's self-esteem you do not enter into temptation with the demon of blasphemy and pride.

54. Pray that you do not enter into the manifest temptations of the senses which Satan knows how to bring upon you, when God permits him, on account of the foolish opinions you have devised.

55. Pray that the [Angel] witness of chastity not withdraw from you and you be tempted in the flames of sin and be separated from him.

56. Pray that you do not enter into the temptation of being contemptuous of anything.

---

[63] Lk 22:28; Acts 14:22.
[64] Mt 20:22, Peshitta.

57. Pray therefore, that you do not enter into the temptations of the soul; namely, those which place the soul in struggle, in doubts and in provocations. But for those of the body, be ready with your whole body and with all your members, and swim with your eyes full of tears so that you may be found to be with your guardian [angel] amidst them. For without temptations God's providence is not perceived, and familiarity with Him is not acquired, and wisdom of spirit is not learned and the love of God is not rooted in the soul.

58. Before being tempted one prays to God as a stranger. But when one has entered tribulations because of his love and has not undergone change, then, as one who has laid obligations on God, he is considered God's housemate and friend, who has contended for the sake of [God's] will against the army of his enemies. This is the meaning of: "Pray lest you enter into temptation."

59. And again: Pray that you do not enter into temptations on account of your pride but rather because you love God, that his power may shine out in you. Pray that you not enter into these temptations because of the folly of your thoughts and your deeds, but that you may be proved a friend of God, and that his power may be glorified in your patience.

60. Concerning the mercifulness of our Lord, which is at this gate, [how] He stretches out his word in proportion to human weakness. Furthermore, this opportunity He uses mercifully. If you consider the things of the body, you see that God gives heed to the infirmity of nature, lest perhaps on account of the wretchedness of the body, we would not find fortitude before the violence of the temptations when they occur, and because of this also fall from truth when we are overcome by afflictions. Therefore He commands us that insofar as possible one should not willfully let oneself fall into temptation. And not only this, but also, you should pray earnestly that

you not be found in temptation by chance,[65] if it is possible to please God without temptation.

61.   But if it is necessary on account of great virtue that temptations assail, even the most terrible, and if only when one accepts them is it possible to achieve virtue, in this case it is not right for us to be partial to ourselves or to anyone. Not even because of fear may you abandon that great event upon which hangs the life of your soul, taking to disguise weakness: "Pray that you enter not into temptation." These are those of whom it is said that they sin secretly against the commandments.

62.   And again, if a person happens to violate one of God's commandments, whether it be the state of chastity, or the habit of holiness, or the confession of faith, or testimony concerning God's word, or the attentive guarding of the other precepts of the Law—there is no way that he not fall if he shrinks from temptations. Now then with full confidence one must despise the body and entrust oneself to God and go forth in the name of the Lord. And that One who was with Joseph in the land of Egypt and was a witness of his chastity,[66] and with Daniel in the pit of lions,[67] and with Ananias and his companions in the fiery furnace,[68] and near Jeremiah in the pit of mire and delivering him[69] and letting him find mercy in the midst of the camp of the Chaldeans,[70] and was with Peter in prison and brought him out through closed doors,[71] and with Paul in the synagogues of the Jews[72]— in sum, He who in every generation was near his servants

---

[65]Mk 13:33.
[66]See Gen 37ff.
[67]Cf. Dan 6:17-24.
[68]Cf. Dan 3:49-50, LXX.
[69]Cf. Jer 38.
[70]Jer 39:11ff.
[71]Acts 12:6-11.
[72]Cf. Acts 13.

in every place and region, and manifested in them his
strength and glorified them and kept them in great wonder
so that they saw his salvation openly at the time of their
tribulations—He will strengthen and guard this person in
the midst of tempests which hem him in. Let him then
prevail against the invisible enemy and his hosts with
the zeal of the Maccabees and like the other holy prophets
and apostles and martyrs and confessors and solitaries
who have kept the divine laws and the commandments
of the Spirit in dreadful places and in grievous and fear-
ful temptations and who have cast down the world and
the body behind them and have clung to the truth and
were not overcome by the force that pressed upon both
body and soul, but were heroically triumphant—in brief,
whose names are inscribed in the book of life until the
coming of our Lord. Their deeds are preserved in the
book by God's will for our instruction and encouragement, according to the testimony of the blessed Apostle,[73]
that we may become wise through them and learn the
way of God when we put their stories, like living icons,
before the eyes of our mind, and take an example from
them and conform the ways of our ascetic life to them,
like the men of old.

63.   To the soul endowed with reason the words of
God are sweet, like succulent food which fattens the
body is to the palate of those who are healthy.

64.   The stories of the just are desirable to the hearing of the innocent as constant watering is to young plants.

66.   May attention to the economy of God which
ministered to those of former times, be reckoned by you
as precious medicine for weak eyes; and let the memory
of it stay with you at all times of the day. Meditate,
apply your mind, and learn wisdom from it, that you
may be able to receive into your soul with honor, the

---

[73]Cf. Rom 15:4; Heb. 11; 1 Cor 10:11.

memory of the greatness of God, and find eternal life
for yourself in Jesus Christ, the mediator between God
and mankind and the Uniter in his two natures.[74] It is
He who, while legions of angels are not able to contemplate the splendor which surrounds the throne of his
glory, for your sake is made manifest to the world as
"the most despised and humiliated of men, without form
or splendor."[75] And, though his invisible nature did not
fall under the perception of creatures, with the veil of
our limbs He fulfilled his divine economy for the redemp-
tion of the life of all.

67. "This is the one through whom God has purified
many peoples";[76] and, "The Lord has laid on Him the
sins of us all,"[77] according to the word of Isaiah. "The
Lord was pleased to humiliate Him and to afflict Him."[78]
"Sin has been placed in Him while He did not know
sin."[79] To Him, for his Divine Economy in all genera-
tions for our sake, be glory and praise and thanksgiving
and adoration by all, now and always and forever and
ever. Amen.

[74] 1 Tim 2:5.
[75] Is 53:2-3.
[76] Is 52:15, Peshitta.
[77] Is 53.6.
[78] Is 53.10.
[79] 2 Cor 5:21.

FOURTH DISCOURSE

1. The soul that loves God is at rest in God alone.

2. First loosen external bonds from yourself and then be solicitous to bind your heart to God.

3. Liberation from matter precedes the bond with God.

4. One offers bread for food to an infant after it is weaned from milk. A man who wishes to grow in God must first wean his soul from the world, as an infant is weaned from its mother's breasts.[80]

5. Bodily labors precede the work of the soul, just as in generation the creation of the body preceded that of the soul.[81]

6. Indeed, one who does not have the labors of the body does not have the labors of the soul. For the latter are born from the former, as an ear of corn from a bare grain. One who does not have the work of the soul is also deprived of the gifts of the Spirit.

7. Temporary sufferings for the sake of truth cannot be compared to that delight prepared for those who labor for virtue.[82]

8. As the weeping of sowing is followed by sheaves of joy,[83] so joy follows labors done for the sake of God.

---

[80]Ps 131:2; cf. 1 Cor 3:1-2.
[81]Cf. Gen 2:7.
[82]Rom 8:18.

Bread [earned through] sweat is sweet to the workman. Labors for the sake of righteousness are sweet to the heart that has received the knowledge of Christ.

9. Endure contempt and humiliation with a virtuous mind for the sake of confidence of heart before God. For every hard word which a person endures with discernment, except for when [he is] the cause of the offense, he will receive a crown of thorns on his head for the sake of Christ, blessed be He. And one also will be crowned at a time that one does not know.

10. One who wittingly flees from praise senses within himself the hope of the future world.

11. One who promises abandonment of the world and quarrels with men on account of things, so as not to be deprived of his pleasure, is completely blind. He has left the whole world voluntarily and quarrels for a part of it!

12. The mind of one who flees from the pleasures of this life beholds the future world.

13. One who lays hold of possessions is the slave of passions. Do not count only gold and silver as possessions but all things you lay hold of with willful desire.

14. A person who cuts off entanglements because he fears passions is truly wise.

15. Without the constant practice of virtue true knowledge cannot be found.

16. Knowledge of life is acquired not by bodily works alone but when we set as goal for these works the cutting off of all the passions of the mind. One who toils without discernment will also easily succumb to the occasions of sin when they present themselves to him.

17. Never praise one who labors with his body but is relaxed and permissive in his senses, that is, whose ears and mouth are open and whose eyes wander.

18. When you set for your soul the goal of doing

---

[83]Cf. Ps 126:5-6.

works of mercy, educate it not to lay hold of justice at other gates[84] lest you appear to work with one hand and scatter with the other. For there compassion is necessary but here magnanimity.

19.   Consider the forgiveness of your debtors in these things as a work of righteousness. Then you will see peace exult in your mind from two sides: namely when you are above propriety and justice in your way and you yield to freedom in all things.

20.   Indeed one of the saints[85] when speaking on these things says: "If the merciful one is not just he is blind." This means that from riches [acquired] in righteousness and from his own labors he should provide for others and not from the gains of falsehood and oppression and cruelty and tricks.

21.   Likewise, in another place, this man also instructs: "If you sow among the poor you must sow what is your own because that from strangers is more bitter than weeds."

22.   But I say, if the merciful one is not also beyond justice, he is not merciful. That is, not only from his own part will he be merciful to others, but also he will endure injustice gladly and voluntarily. He will also not establish and seek full justice in his dealing with his companion but will be merciful to him; because when he overcomes justice with mercy he will weave for himself a crown, not of those who are just according to the Law, but of the perfect according to the New Covenant.

23.   Also the old Law commands one to give to the poor from one's own [possessions], to cover the naked when one sees them, to love one's neighbor as oneself

---

[84]The biblical practice consisted in dealing justice at the gates of the city. Cf. Josh 20:4; Amos 5:12; Ruth 4:1,11.

[85]See St Neilos the Ascetic, *Senteniae*, nn. 43 and 42 in PG 79, 1244c.

and not to defraud or deceive. But the perfect way of life of the new Law commands thus: "If someone takes what belongs to you, do not require it back; and whatever he asks of you, give him."[86] And not only must you bear gladly the tyranny of possessions and the other things that are outside of you, but also you must give of yourself for your kindred.

24. He is merciful who shows compassion to his neighbor not only with gifts, but also when he hears or sees anything that causes suffering to someone, he does not prevent his heart from burning. And even if he is struck a blow by his brother, he does not presume to retaliate against him with so much as a word and cause him mental suffering.[87]

25. Honor the labors of the vigil that you may find consolation close by within your soul. Persevere in reading, in stillness, and you will be led toward wonder at every moment. Love poverty constantly that your mind may be collected from dispersion.

26. Hate opulence that you may be preserved from confusion of mind.

27. Break off from the multitude and take care of your way of life, that your soul may be delivered from the dispersion of its inner quiet.

28. Love chastity lest you be ashamed at the time of petition before Him who ordains the struggle.

29. Acquire excellency in your way of life that your soul may exult in prayer and joy be kindled in your mind at the remembrance of death.

30. Stand firm with regard to small things lest you drive away great ones.

31. Do not hesitate before labors lest you be ashamed when you come together with all your companions.

---

[86]Lk 6:30, Peshitta.
[87]Cf. Mt 5:39.

32. Bear your labor with knowledge lest it cause you to cease from the entire course.[88]

33. Do not be lacking in provisions lest they leave you by yourself in the middle of the way and depart.[89]

34. Acquire freedom in your way of life that you may be free from confusion.

35. Do not seize your freedom as a pretext for pleasures,[90] lest you become the slave of slaves.

36. Cherish poverty in your way of life that the ideas which look in the direction of exaltation of the heart and licentiousness may be subdued at once. It is not possible that one who loves elegance acquire a humiliated mind. For the heart within and the outer habits necessarily proceed together. Who can acquire a chaste mind while he cultivates luxury? Or who can attempt to contemplate external glory and acquire humiliated thoughts within himself? Who is the one extravagant in his outward appearance and dissipated in his bodily parts, who is also chaste in his heart and pious in his thoughts? When the mind is guided by the senses it is nourished with them on the food of animals. But when the senses are guided by the mind they are nourished with it on the food of angels.[91]

37. Vain glory is a servant of fornication but when it exists in the ascetic life it serves pride. To humility is joined restraint but to love of praise, dissipation. The former indeed through continuous recollection arrives at contemplations and arms the soul for chastity. But this latter through continuous wandering of the mind, gathers provisions through contact with things and defiles the heart.

---

[88]Cf. 1 Cor 9:24.

[89]Cf. Mt 25:1ff; see also interpretation of the parable of the ten virgins in the Macarian Homilies 4:6 (tr. A. J. Mason).

[90]Cf. Gal 5:13; 1 Pt 2:16.

[91]Ps 78:25.

38. For love of glory touches on the nature of things with lust and inflames the mind by means of lascivious thoughts. Whereas humility, by contemplation of these natures, restrains spiritually and stirs up those who possess it toward the praise [of God].

39. Do not compare then, all the powers and signs that are performed in the whole world with the fact that a person abides wittingly in stillness.

40. Cherish the leisure of stillness more than satisfying the hungry of the world, or converting a multitude of peoples from error to the worship of God. Let it be more excellent in your eyes to free your soul from the bonds of sin than to liberate the oppressed from those who subject their bodies.

41. Be reconciled with your soul in concord with the triad which is in you, body—soul—spirit, rather than reconcile by your teaching those at enmity.

42. Love ignorance of speech together with the knowledge of experience from within, more than spouting forth a Gihon[92] of teaching with keenness of mind and an accumulation of hearsay and writing.

43. Take care to awaken your soul from the deadness of passions, toward the movement of its impulses which are in God, rather than to raise from death those who have died a natural death.

44. Many have performed miracles and have raised the dead and have labored for the erring and done great signs, and they have drawn many to God through admiration for them because of what is in their hands; but afterwards these who saved others have fallen into shameful and contemptible passions. And after they had given life to others they brought death to themselves and turned and caused those others to sin by the contradiction which was made manifest in their works. In that while they

---

[92]Cf. Gen 2:13.

were still sick in their soul they did not take care about their own healing. But they let themselves be cast into the sea of the world to heal the souls of others while they themselves were still sick. And they have deprived themselves of hope in God, in this sense that I have said, because the weakness of their senses was not able to oppose the rays of things which usually excite the intensity of the passions in those who still are in need of vigilance. I mean the sight of women and comfort and money and things, and the passion for primacy and arrogance over others.

45. Let yourself be despised by fools on account of ignorance and not by the wise because of shamelessness.

46. Become poor for the sake of humiliation and do not grow rich for the sake of impudence.

47. Put disputants to shame by the power of your virtues, not by means of a command; and confound the boldness of the disobedient with the gentleness of your lips, not with shouts.

48. Shame the lustful by the sobriety of your way of life, and those who are boldly sensual by the modesty of your eyes which are concentrated within you in tranquility.

49. Consider yourself a stranger[98] wherever you go all your days, that you may be able to flee the great harm generated by excessive familiarity.

50. Always think of your soul as knowing nothing, that you may be preserved from the reprehensible things which the supposition that you are capable of directing others stirs in you.

51. Let your mouth be constant in blessings and no one's abuse will ever fall on you. Insult generates insult and blessing, blessing.

52. Always consider yourself as needing instruction

---

[98]Cf. Heb 11:13.

so that you may be found wise throughout your life.

53. Do not transmit to others as your own that rule of life to which you have not yet attained lest you be ashamed of your soul, and from the comparison with your way of life your lie will be revealed. But even if you speak on what is fitting, speak as a pupil and not authoritatively, by first humiliating yourself and showing that you are less than [your listener]. Indeed you will give to your listeners an example of humility; moreover, the hearing of your words will stimulate them in the race toward works and you will be honored in their eyes.

54. As much as possible speak about things such as these with tears, so that it may be useful for your soul and for your companions, and draw grace to you.

55. If by Christ's grace you have reached the delight of the mysteries of created things that are seen, which is the first summit of knowledge, arm your soul against the spirit of blasphemy; for without armour you will not stand firm in this place without being killed suddenly in secret by the seducers. Your armour is fasting and those tears which you shed in continual bowing down; and that you beware of reading the writings of those who divide the minds of the worshippers with the aim indeed of destruction, that is to say, arming the spirit of blasphemy more and more against the soul.

56. When your belly is full do not dare to scrutinize lest you regret it. Understand what I say: in a full belly there is not knowledge of the mysteries of God. Chant often, indeed insatiably, from the writings which treat of the Divine Economy, which have been composed by holy men and which manifest the purpose of the variety of the works of God in the creation of the different substances of the world; so that your intellect be strengthened by them and you receive luminous impulses from their subtle penetration. Thus may your mind travel with limpidity toward the goal of a true statement about the

creation of the world, according to the praiseworthy, wise intelligence of the Creator of the substances.

57. Read the two Testaments which God has constituted for the knowledge of the whole world, so that by the power of his Divine Economy, [the world] may be provided with food in every generation, and be enveloped in wonder.

58. Readings such as these are very useful for this purpose. Let your reading be done in complete stillness, when you are freed from excessive care of the body and the tumult of affairs. Then [the reading] will give your soul a delightful taste of sweet understandings, beyond the senses, that the soul perceives within by being constant in the readings. Do not reckon words of experience as the babbling of those who peddle words lest you remain in darkness until the end of your life, because deprived of their advantage you will grope as in the night in times of struggle, not to mention being cast down into one of the pits having an appearance of truth.

59. This will be the sign for you when you have drawn near to entering into that region [of truth]. When grace has begun to open your eyes to perceive an exact vision of these things, then your eyes will begin to shed tears until your cheeks are washed by their abundance, and the fervor of the senses will be slowed that they may profitably be restrained within you. If there is one who teaches you other than this do not believe him. But you are not permitted to seek another indication from the body besides tears as a manifest sign of the perception of truth, unless in the silence of the activity of the members of the body. This happens when the mind is raised above existing things, and the body ceases from tears and perception and any movement except physical vitality. For that knowledge does not submit to assuming the forms of things of the sensible world as associated figuratively in the vision of the mind.

60. "Whether in the body or out of the body, I do not know; God knows"; and Paul said this, "because he has heard ineffable things."[94]

61. All that is heard with the ears can be spoken. But [Paul] did not understand with perceptible sounds nor with a vision of material images of sensible things, but with impulses of the mind, in being caught up away from the body, the will having no part with it.

62. Eye indeed has never seen its like, and the ear has not heard its equal; and he never dreamed to call to mind, through the memory of the kinds of knowledge, the likeness of what his heart has seen, namely that which God has prepared to manifest to the pure in heart when they are dead to the world.[95] It is not corporeal vision that is received through the eyes of flesh with its coarse distinctions, and not the illusions which are formed by them in the mind derivatively; but it is simple contemplation of the things of the intellect and of faith, which defies dismemberment and clear division and shows the primary images.

63. Fix your gaze on the orb of the sun according to the degree of your visual power, only to enjoy its rays and not to investigate its course, lest you be deprived even of your modest vision. If you find honey eat as much as is sufficient for you,[96] that when you are filled you do not vomit it. The nature of the soul is a small thing and sometimes [the soul] is presumptuous in desiring to learn what is higher than its nature.

64. Many times in the course of reading or contemplating, the soul apprehends various things; yet the measure of its knowledge is much less in comparison with what it has found. But how far does its knowledge penetrate? Until its deliberations are clothed with shak-

---

[94] 2 Cor 12:2-4.
[95] Cf. 1 Cor 2:9.
[96] Cf. Prov 25:16.

ing and trembling. And again through fear it hastens to turn back when it presumes to venture into fiery things.[97]

65. Fear indeed restrains the soul because of the power of these things. And discernment, indeed, in silence, indicates to the soul's mind that it not venture lest it die. Do not seek what is hard for you; nor pursue what is grievous for you. "Perceive what is in your power and do not venture toward hidden things." Adore therefore and praise in silence and confess incomprehensibility. Because enough has been manifested to you, do not be indignant about the rest of His works. And as it is not good to eat much honey, neither is it [good] to investigate glorious words;[98] lest, desiring to see from a great distance before we have drawn near, we succumb from the interminable way and even be without the power of sight and be hurt. Sometimes fantasies usurp the place of truth, for when the intellect is weary of comprehension its accuracy errs. Wise Solomon spoke well: "As a breached city without walls, thus is the one who is not patient."[99]

66. It is not necessary to roam heaven and earth after God or to send our mind to seek Him in different places.[100] Purify your soul, O son of man, remove from yourself the thought of memories which are outside nature; hang the veil of chastity and humility before your impulses. By means of these you will be able to find Him who is within you. "For mysteries are revealed to the humble."[101]

67. If you have given yourself to the work of prayer,

---

[97]"Fiery things" seems to refer to the words of Scripture. See Deut 33:2 (Hebrew text): "... from his right hand went forth a fiery law for them." Also, Patristic and Rabbinical exegesis comments on the word of God as fire in reference to this verse.
[98]Prov 25:27, Peshitta.
[99]Prov 25:28, Peshitta.
[100]Cf. Deut 30:11-14.
[101]Cf. Lk 10:21; Sir 3:21, Peshitta.

purifier of the mind, and to constancy in night vigils so
as to acquire a mind clad with light, withdraw yourself
from the appearances of the world and cut yourself off
from conversation. Do not seek habitually to receive your
friend within your cell, not even with the pretext of
virtue, except the one who has your same purpose and
shares the secrets of your way of life. If you fear distraction and that secret mental discourse which usually
arises in the soul without our seeking it, cut yourself off
from outward discourse, too.

68.   Add virtues to your prayer, that your soul may
see the splendid manifestation of truth. As much as the
heart finds peace from the memories of created things, so
much will your mind receive [the gift of] wonder for the
understanding of the sayings [of Scripture]. The soul is
easily accustomed to change one occupation for another,
if we show a little care and take the trouble.

69.   Burden [the soul] with the labor of reading the
Scriptures which make known the narrow ways of the
ascetic life and of contemplation, as well as stories of the
saints; that you may exchange one habit for another even
if in the beginning your soul does not feel pleasure because of the thick darkness and confusion of present
memories. Then when you arise for prayer and for the
office, instead of musings upon things of the world, ideas
from Scripture will be imprinted in the mind. And with
these, the memory of what it already has seen and heard
will be effaced from it. In this way your mind will come
to purity. This is what is said: "The soul is plied with
reading when it comes to prayer and by reading it is
illuminated in prayer." That is, instead of external distraction, the soul finds [in Scripture] material for different
kinds of prayer, and true understandings will come to
mind because of the marvelous memories from [Scripture],
so that often at these moments, the power of contemplation [derived] from Scripture silences and astonishes even

during prayer, and [the one who prays] is made to stand without movement. That [power] also at the appointed time cuts off prayer through pleasure, as I have said, imparting stillness to the heart and silencing its impulses through a pause of the members of soul and body.

70. Those who have experienced this matter in their souls and have been within its mysteries, know what I am saying. They have not received it from the teaching of others nor have they snatched it from writings which so often are found to falsify the truth.

71. A full stomach loathes examining spiritual questions as a harlot loathes speaking of chastity.

72. A stomach full of distress abhors succulent food. And a mind full of the world cannot approach any examination of divine works.

73. Fire does not blaze among fresh wood,[102] and enthusiasm for God does not break forth into flames in a heart that loves comfort.

74. A harlot does not persist in alliance with one man nor does a soul which is tied to many things abide in the love of spiritual teaching.

75. Just as one who has never seen the sun with his own eyes is not able to imagine its light in his mind only from hearing about it, or to receive an image of something in his soul, or to perceive the beauty of its beams of light, so, he who in his soul has not felt the taste of spiritual work, and in his ascetic life has not remained within the experience of its mysteries so as to receive in his mind an image which resembles truth, is not able from human teaching or the instruction which is in writings to find true conviction in his soul or to attain to the essence of the matter.

76. If you possess anything left over from the daily nourishment, go and give it to the poor and come offer

---

[102]Cf. Lk 23:31.

prayer with confidence. That is, speak with God as a
son with his father.

77. There is nothing which brings the heart as near
to God as mercy, and nothing which gives peace to the
mind as much as voluntary poverty. Many will reprove
you as ignorant because of your openhandedness and your
liberality without measure as a sign of the fear of God;
and on account of your abstinence they will say that
you are not wise or mentally stable. If a man is riding a
horse and stretches out his hand, do not withdraw your
hand from him, which holds what his need truly requires.
For at that time, he is in need as one of the poor. And
when you give, give with a generous eye and make your
countenance cheerful toward him.[103] Give him beyond
what he sought, even what he did not ask. "Cast your
bread on the waters and after a long time you will find
recompense."[104] Do not distinguish between rich and poor,
and do not determine who is worthy and who is not
worthy. For your part treat all men as worthy of goodness, especially because thereby you will stimulate them
to truth. The soul is easily drawn by bodily things to
reflect on the fear of God. Also our Lord shared his
table with publicans and harlots, while not distinguishing
who was unworthy, so as through this to provoke them
to the fear of God. By the sharing of bodily things, He
brought them to the sharing which is in the Siprit. For
this reason consider all men worthy of goodness and
honor, whether they be Jews or infidels or murderers;
all the more so [if] a person is your brother of your same
nature who in ignorance wanders from the truth. When
you do good, do not set for your mind the goal of an
immediate reward and you will be doubly recompensed
by God. If possible [do not do good] even for a reward

---

[103]Cf. Rom 12:8; 2 Cor 9:7.
[104]Eccles 11:1.

that is beyond this life, but rather excel for the love of God. The degree of love is deeper even than that of virtuous work for God. And in its mystery it penetrates more deeply than this [work], more intimately than the soul penetrates the body.

78. If you have already set for yourself the goal of poverty, and by the grace of God you have been freed from anxiety and in your renunciation you are above the world, beware lest for love of the poor you yearn to fall back into solicitude for possessions and things, under the pretext of giving alms. Then your soul will again be thrown into tumult, taking from one and giving to another, and you will debase your honor by bending over to persuade men to give you this or that kind of thing, and you will fall again from the height of your mental freedom into concern for earthly things. Your rank is higher than that of those who give alms. I beseech you, do not let yourself be ridiculed. [Almsgiving] is the rule for the education of youth, while poverty is the way of perfection. If you have goods distribute them immediately, but if you do not, do not desire to have them. Purify your dwelling of delicacies and superfluous things; this will necessarily bring you to poverty. For necessity endures many things, which we by choice, when possible, would not consent to endure. Those who have overcome the external strtuggle have also removed inner fear, and there is no longer any compulsion which will lead them against their will by troubling them with strife, before and behind.

79. By outward struggle I mean that which one foolishly excites against one's soul with the senses, that is, by getting and giving, hearing and seeing, talk and the belly; and thus continuously, one after another, one increases the affairs in his soul so that it be blinded by external troubles that meet it, unable to see itself in the secret war which is stirred up, and unable to conquer for

the sake of tranquility that which comes from within.

80.   But if one makes fast the city gates there will be
face to face strife and one will not fear ambushes from
outside the city. Blessed is the one who knows these
things and perseveres in stillness and does not increase his
work there [in stillness], but exchanges all his bodily work
for the labor of prayer, if he is capable; and who passing
from service to service does not associate anything with
the work of God which is prayer and reading, but be-
lieves that while serving God and thinking about Him
night and day he will not lack any of the necessities which
he requires because he does not work for himself.

81.   If someone cannot endure stillness without work,
necessarily he must work but he must take it as a help
and not greedily, and as secondary [to prayer and reading]
and not as a principal commandment. This is for the
weak as it were. Evagrius calls manual labor a hindrance
to the remembrance of God.[105] The Fathers have pre-
scribed work for the needy and despondent and not for
those who are assiduous in the demands of the law.

82.   When God opens your mind from within and
you give yourself to frequent kneelings, do not give your
heart to anxiety about anything even though you are persuaded by demons in secret; and then see and marvel at
what is born in you from these things. Do not compare
any way of life with that of a man throwing himself on
his face day and night before the Cross while his hands
are thrust behind him. If you desire that your fervour
never be dulled and that you not be deprived of tears,
do these things. Blessed are you, O man, if you reflect
on these things that I have told you, and night and day
seek nothing else. Then your light will break as the dawn
and your righteousness will shine forth directly. Then you

---

[105]Cf. Evagrius, *Admonitio Paraenetica* 2, in *Evagriana Syriaca*,
ed. J. Muyldermans (Louvain, 1952), p. 157.

will be like a luxuriant garden and like a spring whose waters do not fail.[106]

83. Behold how many good things are granted to a man by diligence! Sometimes a man is steadfast on his knees at the time of prayer with hands outstretched or extended toward heaven and his head looking on the Cross so that one might say that all his impules and mind are stretched out towards God in supplication. At that time, while the man is [immersed] in these supplications and groanings, a fountain of delight will spring up suddenly in his heart and his limbs will be relaxed. His eyes closed and his face covered, his thoughts will be transformed so that not even his knees are able to stay on the ground before the exultation of that good which swells up through his whole body.

84. Understand, O man, what you are reading. Can one truly know these things from ink? Or does the taste of honey pass over the palate of the reader from books?

85. If you are not careful you will not find. If you do not knock fervently and keep patient watch at the door you will not be answered.[107]

86. Who is it that will hear these things and yearn for external righteousness, if not the one who is unable to endure the bonds of the cell? But if there is anyone who is not equal to these things, since it is a gift of God that a man should remain inside the door, he should nevertheless not desist from that other part (work of external righteousness), lest he be deprived of both parts of life.

87. Until the outer man has died to the affairs of the world, not only to sin but to every bodily work, and the inner man to importunate memories of bad things, and moreover until the natural impulse is humbled and

---

[106]Is 58:8,11.; cf. Ps 37:6.
[107]Mt 7:7.

the body has almost died through exertion—so that the
sweetness of sin is not strong in the heart—God's Spirit
will not spread its sweetness in man; his limbs will not
be opened to life and divine impulses will not appear in
the soul. And as long as the heart does not desist from
earthly care, except for those necessities that nature
requires of him at the time of his need—although even
these he should leave to God's providence—drunkenness
of the Spirit cannot arise in him. He will not perceive
that madness for which the Apostle was mocked: "The
multitude of writings have made him mad."[108]

88. But this I have not said to take away hope, as
if unless a man reach the depth of perfection the grace
of God will not be given to him nor consolation come
to him.

89. Truly when a person rejects evil things and becomes wholly estranged from them and cleaves to good
things,[109] in a short time he will feel the advantage. And
if he is but a little diligent, he will find the consolation
of the forgiveness of sins in himself, and will be made
worthy of grace and receive many good things.

90. But this is little in comparison with the one who
is completely estranged from the world and has found
in himself that sign of future blessings and has obtained
that for the sake of which Christ obtained us.

To Him and to his Father and to the Holy Spirit be
glory and praise forever and ever. Amen.

---

[108]Cf. Acts 26:24.
[109]Cf. Ps 34:15.

FIFTH DISCOURSE

1. God has increased man's honor by the double instruction He has given him. On all sides He has opened a door for him that he may enter into knowledge.

2. Seek from nature a true witness concerning your soul and you will not err. But if you go astray from there learn from a second witness and it will place you on the way from which you strayed.

3. A wandering heart cannot avoid straying; Wisdom does not open its gate before it.

4. The one who is able to understand correctly what is the future final dignity of all mankind does not seek another teacher concerning the wretchedness of the world.

5. The first writing which you are given by God for rational beings is the nature of creation.[110] But instruction in ink was added after transgression. The one who does not withdraw from the occasions of sin voluntarily is drawn toward sin involuntarily.

6. Occasions for sin are wine and woman, riches and a healthy body. It is not that these things in and of themselves are to be designated as sin, but on account of human weakness and the unlawful use of them. Indeed, by them more than anything else, nature can easily be prone to various sins; concerning them, greater vigilance is required of it.

---

[110]Cf. Rom 1:20; see also Evagrius *Praktikos,* ch. 92.

7. If you remember continually and know exactly that you are weak, you will never overstep the limits of vigilance.

8. Poverty is more despised among persons than anything else but before God even more despised than it is pride of heart and a scornful mind.

9. Among men wealth is honored, but by God a humble soul.

10. When you wish to begin [to practice] one of the virtues, first prepare your soul, lest by the evil things which come as a consequence, you be made to doubt the truth.

11. When the evil one happens to see someone beginning [to practice] one of the virtues with the enthusiasm of faith he lays upon him violent and terrible temptations, so that when he is terrified by them the love in his mind grows dim and is no longer fervent to approach the works of God. Therefore, through fear of the temptations which accompany good works, good works are not practiced by anyone.

12. But you, prepare your soul, that bravely and mightily you may resist the evils which accompany virtues; and then begin!

13. If you do not expect evil things, do not begin [to practice] virtue. One who doubts the Lord is persecuted by his own shadow; and in time of satiety he is hungry. In time of peace his ruin is grievous. But the heart of one who trusts in God will be strengthened, and his honor will be manifest before the multitudes and his glory before his enemies. God's commandments are better than all the earth's treasures.[111] One who has God's laws in his heart will find the Lord within them.

14. One who passes the night with the thought of Him makes of God a housemate; and one who earnestly

---

[111]Cf. Ps 119:127.

desires the will of God will find the Watchers on high[112] to be his teachers.

15. The one who trembles before sin will proceed without stumbling, even through terrible places. In time of thick darkness he will find light within himself.

16. The Lord will guard the ways of the one who trembles before sin; mercy will anticipate his falls.

17. The one whose offenses are small in his eyes will fall into even graver ones, to be requited sevenfold.

18. Sow alms in humility and you will reap in the court of justice.

19. With that whereby you have lost good things, with the same you must again acquire them. If you owe God a penny somewhere, He will not accept a pearl in its place; in that case the penny is required.

20. If you have cast chastity away from you do not leave fornication in its place, giving alms instead of it: God will not accept this from you. In the place proper to holiness, He requires sanctity.

21. If you have not done wrong to the poor, do not allow greedy possession to enter in. While you abstain from bread, do not permit iniquity in its place or you will have to struggle with something else. Wrong [doing] is eradicated with mercy and renunciation. You have left the sucker [on the plant] while you struggle with something else, according to the word of the great teacher Mar Ephrem.

22. "During summer be careful not to fight the heat in winter clothes."

23. Thus, everyone from that injustice which he sows will reap its contrary, and he will fight each illness with its own remedy.

24. Now you are consumed by envy, but you fight

---

[112]In Syriac literature, angels are frequently referred to as "Watchers," cf. Dan 4:10-23.

against sleep! While sin is green, eradicate it lest it cover all the earth. The one who neglects evil as if it were a small thing, at length will find it a grievous master, and he will run before it in chains. But the one who persists from the beginning, will dominate it easily. Whoever endures injustice gladly because victory is in his hand has received this perceptible consolation of his faith from God.

25. The one who bears slander with humility has arrived at perfection. The angels will be amazed at this.

26. There is no virtue more difficult or greater than that.

27. Do not believe yourself strong until you enter into temptations and find your mind unwavering in the midst of them. And in all things you should so try your soul.

28. Acquire glory through the faith of your heart, that you may tread on the neck of your enemies and find your mind humble. Do not rely on your strength, lest you be abandoned to the weakness of your nature and in your fall learn your weakness. [Do not rely] on your knowledge lest you be surrounded by thoughts of secret stratagems and be confused.

29. Acquire a humble tongue and shame will never fall upon you. Acquire pleasant lips and you will be found a friend to everyone. Do not boast of anything with your tongue, lest your shame be double when you are found in what is contrary, because there is no creature exempt from change.

30. Whatever you boast of before men God carefully changes so that you will have an occasion for humility. You must attribute all things to the knowledge of God, and not believe that there is truth in creatures. When you attain this, your eyes will be fixed on Him at all times.

31. Divine Providence surrounds all persons at all times, but it is not visible except to those who have

purified their souls of sin and think about God at all times. To these it is luminously revealed at that time; because when they have undergone great temptations for the sake of truth, then they receive the faculty to perceive sensibly as if with eyes of flesh also when necessary, even palpably, according to the kind and cause of the temptation, as if for greater encouragement.

32. So it was with Jacob and Joshua son of Nun, Hananiah and his companions, Peter and others to whom the form of a man appeared to encourage them and to console their faith.[113]

33. And if you say that these are effects of Divine Providence and universal matters, let the holy martyrs be encouragement to you. They who were sometimes many together, or each one in different places, have suffered for God. There was a hidden power with them by which they withstood the tearing asunder of their bodily parts with irons, and tortures of all kinds, torments beyond nature. Sometimes the holy angels appeared openly to them. This [was] that everyone might know that God's providence is toward those who bear sufferings for His sake for whatever reason—for their own encouragement and the shame of their torturers. For as much as those were made glorious by such visions, these [adversaries] were tormented by their endurance.

34. What shall we say about the many solitaries, strangers and true mourners who have made the desert an inhabited land and a place for the hosts of angels who have joined with them because of the equality of their ways of life.[114] As true fellow-servants of one Lord they mingled with the multitudes from on high in their places of meeting. These are the ones who all their lives

---

[113]Cf. Gen 32:24-29; Josh 5:13-15; Dan 3:49-50, 92(LXX); Acts 12:6-11.
[114]Cf. Ps 34:7.

have loved solitude and have made caves and crags their
dwelling places, and who have gladly endured loneliness
and the desert for the love of God. And because they
forsook the earth and loved heaven as the angels do,
truly the angels have not hidden themselves from their
sight.

35. But sometimes they taught them concerning the
ascetic life. And at times they answered their queries concerning other things of which they asked. Sometimes when
they wandered in the desert, [the angels] showed them the
way. And sometimes they delivered them from temptations. Sometimes they saved them from the midst of sudden
peril which they came upon unwittingly.

36. Such as a serpent, or falling from a precipice, or
some stone falling suddenly from high up with a rush.

37. And sometimes also in the vehemence of the open
battles of Satan, [the angels] showed themselves openly
to them and clearly indicated that they were sent for their
aid and offered them encouragement with their words.

38. At times they also cured their diseases and by
the touch of their hands healed injuries that happened
to them from whatever cause. Yet other times, to bodies
wearied by the lack of nourishment, the angels gave
supernatural force by their words or by a sudden touch
of the hand, and mysteriously conferred strength on fallen
nature. Sometimes they brought food to them: warm bread
and olives, indeed to some, various fruits. To some of them
they revealed the time of their death.

39. How much there is for me to recount concerning
the love of the holy angels for our race and the great
care they show to the righteous; as older brothers who
tend and guard their younger brothers!

40. All of these things are so that everyone may be
assured how near God is to his friends, and how much
care He shows those who entrust their lives into his
hands and follow Him with a limpid heart.

41.   If you are sure of this, and you believe in God's care for you, you must not be concerned about your body, nor even be anxious to guide your soul by means of a strategy.

42.   But if you are doubtful about this and need to be anxious for your soul apart from God, you are the most wretched of all persons. What [use] even for you to live? Cast your care on God[115] that you may be strengthened against all fear.[116]

43.   He who has once entrusted his life to God will dwell in peace of mind.

44.   Without the renunciation of possessions, the soul is not freed from confusion of thoughts.

45.   Without stillness of the senses, peace of mind is not perceived.

46.   And without entering into temptations, wisdom of the Spirit is not acquired.

47.   Without constant reading [of Scripture], subtlety of thoughts is not learned.

48.   And without peace from thoughts, the mind is not moved by hidden mysteries.

49.   Without the confidence of faith, no one will rashly let his soul go into the midst of terrible and difficult things.

50.   Without actually direct experience of God's providence, the heart is not able to confide in God. And unless the soul tastes suffering for the sake of Christ, it will not share in knowledge with Him.

51.   Deem that one a man of God who with his great compassion always stands on the side of poverty.

52.   The one who does good to the poor will find God a provider. And the one who suffers want for love of Him will find in God a great treasure.

53.   God does not have need of anything, but He re-

---

[115]Ps 55:23.
[116]Prov 3:25.

joices when one serves or honors his image (in man)
for his sake.

54.   If anyone asks something of you and you have it,
do not say in your heart: "I will leave it for myself because
I will be better served by it," or "I will let him depart
now, God will provide for him through another; this I
lay aside for myself." Do not say this! For this is how
unjust men think, and people who do not know God
reckon [thus] and dwell on these thoughts. However, a
righteous person does not give his honor to another nor
does he let an opportunity for doing good pass by. By
all means God will pour forth on that one in another
way whenever He knows that he is afflicted. For God
does not abandon anyone. But in that moment you have
let God's honor depart from you and thrust his grace
from you.

55.   But rejoice when you have [something], and give,
and say: "Glory to you, O God, who have granted me
also to be able to comfort someone!"

56.   And when you have nothing rejoice even more,
while thanking God at length with many acknowledge-
ments and saying: "I thank you, O God, for granting me
this honor of becoming poor for your sake and making
me worthy to taste the suffering of sickness and poverty
that you have put on the path of your commandments,
such as the saints who walked by this way have tasted."

57.   And when you are ill say: "Blessed are those who
have found the purpose set by God in these things which
He inflicts for our profit." God brings illness for the
health of the soul.

58.   One of the saints once said: "I have noticed that
when a solitary does not serve God well and is not diligent
in his works, certainly God will send him some temptation to reflect on lest he be completely idle, and through
much idleness the mind turn aside to think on these

things of the left.[117] So whenever he is not willing to think about virtue, the fact of the temptations obliges him to think on it, and not to think idle thoughts. God does this to everyone whom He loves.[118] When He sees that the person has begun to be negligent in His works, He sends him great suffering to make him wise and to chastise him. Therefore, even when such as these call again to Him, He delays and does not hasten to save them until they are weary and they recognize that negligence has caused them to endure these things.

59.   "When you spread forth your hands, I will hide my eyes from you; and even though you make many prayers, I will not listen."[119]

60.   Even though this was said for others, by all means it may be said for those who abandon the way.

61.   But, if God is so merciful, why must we earnestly knock at his door in distrtess and pray, to have Him turn away from our petition? [Scripture] says: "Behold the hand of the Lord is not too short to save; nor his ear hard of hearing. But your iniquities have made a separation between you and God and your sins have turned his face from you, so that he does not hear."[120]

62.   Remember the Lord at all times and He will remember you when evil approaches you. He has made your nature a receptacle of accidents and in the world in which He has created you and placed you, He has multiplied the causes of the accidents and temptations. And He has made your nature a small receptacle of these things. Evil things are not far from you, nor are they few. When He makes a sign they spring up against you from within you, and from under your feet and from the place where

---

[117]Cf. Evagrius, *Chapters on Prayer*, ch. 72.
[118]Cf. Heb 12:6.
[119]Is 1:15.
[120]Is 59:1-2.

you are standing. But as one eyelid is near the other, so temptations are near to the children of men.

63.   God has wisely ordained these things of yours in this way for your own profit that you may continually knock at his door, and through the fear of sorrowful events his memory may constantly come to your mind. Then you will be near to God in constant petition and you will be sanctified by the continual memory of Him in your heart.

64.   When you invoke Him and He answers you, you will know that your saviour is God.[121] And you will be aware of your God as the One who created you, your provider and keeper, because He has made two worlds for your sake: one as it were for your instruction as a school of brief duration, and the other as the house of your Father and your home forever and ever.

65.   [God] has not made you impassible so that you should desire divine rank and inherit what Satan inherited.

66.   And He has not made you inerrant in your soul lest you be as those having bound natures,[122] and you acquire your good things and your evil things without profit and without reward, as do other corporeal beings on the earth. For it is manifest to all how many insults and humiliations, together with thanksgivings, are born from passibility and fear and deviation; so that it may also be known that our zeal for righteousness and our turning from evil things are effects of our will. Thus honor and shame are derived from these and will be

---

[121]Cf. Is 49:26.

[122]"Bound natures" is in contrast to "mutability" in the schemata of Theodore of Mopsuestia assumed by Isaac. Mutability, corruptibility, passibility and mortality constitute this aeon. The future world will be one of immutability, incorruptibility, impassibility and immortality. Life in this age becomes a training and time of growth to prepare for the perfect obedience and immutability of the age to come.

imputed to us. On the one hand, in dishonor we are ashamed and we fear, on the other, in honor we give thanks to God and we press onward to do good.

67. [God] has multiplied all these masters for you, lest freed from them because of your not being in need, or your nature not having the capacity to receive them, the removal of fear and painful things should cause you to forget God and to turn aside from Him and seek a multitude of gods. For many who although passible and indigent and having all these scourgings sent against them, but because of a little wealth and fleeting power and precarious health, not only have they devised many gods but in their madness they have dared to declare themselves gods by nature.

68. Therefore [God] the Lord has preserved you from all these things which afflict you from time to time, lest you go astray and He be angry with you, and He blot you out in punishment from before his presence; not to mention the impiety and sins that flow from good health and lack of fear and ease, even if that which has been previously mentioned (blasphemy) should not occur. Therefore, with sufferings and adversities. He has increased the memory of Him in your heart. And with fear of adversities, He rouses you to the gate of his mercy. By saving you from these [adversities], He sows in you reasons for loving Him. And when you have found love, He brings you to the honor of sons. He will show you how great is his grace and how faithful his providence to you. Then He will make you perceive the holiness of his glory and the hidden mysteries of the nature of his majesty.

69. How would you have become aware of these things if you had not had adversities? Through these the love of God increases in the soul more and more: namely, by the understanding of His goodness and the memory of the various forms of his providence.

'70. All of these good things are generated for you

by sufferings, if you know how to give thanks.

71.   Therefore, remember God, so that He may remember you continually. And when He remembers you and saves you, you will receive all these blessings.

72.   Do not forget Him in your vain distractions, lest He also forget you in your temptations.

73.   In prosperity, be near to [God] and be obedient, that in adversity you may be able to speak freely with Him, because of having been constantly with Him in your heart through prayer.

74.   For all the time you are with Him, sit before Him with your mind on Him and his memory in your heart, lest when you see Him after a long interval you be ashamed to speak to Him with confidence.

75.   Great confidence is born from much constancy [of rapport]. [This] constancy toward persons happens [through] the body. But toward God it is the soul's reflection and an offering of prayers.

76.   On account of its great intensity, this reflection is sometimes mingled with wonder. For the heart of those who seek the Lord will rejoice.[123] Seek the Lord, O sinners, and be strengthened in your thoughts because of hope. And seek his face through repentance at all times[124] and you will be sanctified by the holiness of his presence and you will be purified of your iniquity.[125] Hasten to the Lord, O sinners; He remits iniquity and removes sins. For He has sworn: "I have no pleasure in the death which the sinner dies,"[126] so that the sinner may repent and live.

77.   "I have spread out my hands all day toward a quarrelsome and disobedient people."[127] And, "Why would

---

[123]Ps 105:3.
[124]Ps 105:4.
[125]Ez 36:25.
[126]Ez 33.11.
[127]Is 65:2.

you want to die, O house of Jacob?"[128] "Turn to me and I will turn to you."[129]

78. By Ezekiel He says: "In the day in which the wicked forsakes his way and turns to the Lord and does what is lawful and right, his sins which he has done will not be remembered but he will indeed live, says the Lord." "So also, when the righteous one abandons his righteousness and sins and commits iniquity, the righteousness that he has done will not be remembered; but I will place a stumbling block before him and if he remains steadfast in the iniquity which he has done, he will die in it."[130]

79. For what reason? "Because the iniquitous one will not stumble on account of his iniquity in the day in which he returns to the Lord. And the righteousness of the righteous does not save him in the day that he sins,"[131] if he builds his edifice on this foundation.

80. And to Jeremiah he spoke in this way: "Take a scroll and write on it everything that I have told you, from the day of Josiah the king of Judah, until today, all the evil things that I have told you I would bring upon this people. Perhaps [everyone] will hear and fear and abandon his evil way and repent and return to me, and I will forgive them their sins."[132] And the sage says: "The one who covers his iniquity will not prosper, but God will have mercy on the one who confesses his sins and turns aside from them."[133]

81. And Isaiah, rich in revelations, said: "Seek the Lord. And when you have found Him, invoke Him. And when He is near, let the sinner abandon his way and the

---

[128]Ez 33:11.
[129]Zech 1:3; Mal 3:7.
[130]Ez 18:26-27; 33:18-19.
[131]Cf. Ez 33:12.
[132]Cf. Jer 36:2ff.
[133]Prov 28:13.

evil man his thoughts, let him turn to me and I will have mercy on him, and [turn] to our God who will abundantly forgive. For my thoughts are not as your thoughts, neither are my ways as your ways."[134] "Why do you [not] spend money[135] for what is not bread and labor for what does not satisfy? Listen attentively to me and eat good things. Come to me and hear me and you will live."[136]

82.   When you have kept the ways of the Lord and done his will, then you may trust in the Lord. "Then you will invoke Him and He will answer you. You will call out and He will say: Here I am.[137] When evil befalls a wicked person, he has no confidence to call out to God. And he is not able to await his salvation because he has forsaken his will in the day of his tranquility. Before you have to contend seek a helper for yourself.[138] Seek a physician for yourself before you are ill. Before grief befalls you, pray. And in time of grief you will find [prayer] and it will respond to you. Before you stumble, pray and seek. Before you make a vow, prepare your offerings, that is to say, your provisions. The ark [of Noah] was prepared in time of peace;[139] one hundred years earlier its wood had been planted. And at [the time of] wrath, the wicked who were secure in their wickedness were troubled, but for the righteous one [the ark] was a refuge.[140] The wicked one keeps his mouth shut during prayer. [Indeed], baseness of conscience takes away confidence from the heart. [But] a steadfast heart lets tears

---

[134]Is 55:6-8, Peshitta.

[135]Bedjan adds "not."

[136]Is 55:2-3; cf. Is 1:19.

[137]Is 58:9.

[138]Cf. Sir 18:19-23.

[139]This comment on Gen 6:14 is found in various Midrashic collections. See Rashi who, though later historically, is an accessible witness to this tradition.

[140]Cf. Gen 6:9.

of joy to fall in supplication. Much voluntary endurance
of injustice purifies the heart. Endurance of injustice
comes from contempt of the world. And if one continues
to bear slander without grieving, it is because his heart
has begun to see the truth. Joy on account of slander and
injustice [borne] voluntarily exult the heart. Only those
whose thoughts are completely dead to the world can
bear slander and injustice gladly. But as for those in
whose thoughts the scent of earthly life is still completely
present, vainglory does not allow them not to become
at once inflamed with anger, or to fall into anxious
thoughts generated by [vainglory].

O, how difficult is this virtue and how splendid it is
before God! One who desires this way of life must go
into exile and migrate from his land. It is difficult for one
to accomplish this sublime virtue in his own land. Only
the superior and the strong are able to bear the grief
which is born from this great way of life while remaining
in the midst of those who know them; or those who in
their lives are dead to this life and have given up their
hope of consolation in this world. As grace is near to
humility, so difficult situations [accompany] pride. The
heart of the Lord is toward the humble, to do good to
them. The face of the Lord is against the haughty to
humiliate them.[141] Humility continuously reaps compassion. But hardness of heart and lack of faith always reap
harsh and unexpected attacks, until suddenly evil rises
against [the haughty] and they are delivered to a speedy end.
Make yourself little in everything in the midst of others,
and [God] will exalt you even above the chiefs of the
people. Make a profound inclination before everyone and
be the first [to offer] a greeting and you will be honored
more than the one who brings gold from Ophir.[142] Be

---

[141]Cf. Ps 34:15ff.
[142]1 Kgs 10:11.

contemptible and foolish in your own eyes and you will see the glory of God within your soul. Where humiliation flourishes, there glory will spring up. If you openly endeavor to be rejected by men, [God] will make your honor great. And if in your heart you are humble, in your heart He will show you his glory. Be despised in your greatness and not great in your contemptibility.

83. Learn to be despised while being filled with the Lord's honor and not to be honored while you are wounded by ulcers from within. Reject honor that you may be honored. Do not cherish it lest you be rejected. If you run after honor it will flee before you. And if you flee from it, it will spring up from where you are hiding, and it will be a herald of your humility to all. If you treat your soul with contempt so that you may be honored, the Lord will put you to shame. But if you despise it for the sake of truth, He will command [his] creatures to praise you. And they will manifest before you the glory of the Creator who from eternity speaks with them, and they will praise you as [they do the] Creator because you are his true image. Who can find a person whose way of life is exalted and [who] is despised among men; and illumined and wise and poor in spirit?[143] Blessed is the one who has humbled his soul in everything for he will be magnified in everything. One who for the love of God is humiliated and makes himself little[144] will be glorified by God. And whoever is hungry and thirsty for His sake, [God] will inebriate him from his goods with that wine whose intoxication never wears off in those who drink it. The one who is naked for his sake, He will clothe him with a cloak of glory.[145] And the one who is poor and needy for His sake, He will confirm in him His true riches for his consolation.

---

[143]Cf. Mt 5:3.
[144]Cf. Mk 9:37.
[145]Cf. Is 61:10; Rev 3:4,5,18.

84. Treat your soul with contempt for the love of God that He may increase your glory, even if you are not conscious of it. Throughout your life, consider yourself a sinner, that through all your life you may be found righteous. Be despised when you are wise, and do not be infatuated with your wisdom. Be simple in your wisdom and do not appear to be wise when you are unlearned. If humility elevates the despised, how much more it will elevate the honored. Flee from praise and you will be praised. Fear pride and you will be exalted. "Pomp has not been assigned to mankind nor pride of heart to those born of women." If you have voluntarily renounced the whole body of the world, do not contend with anyone over small parts of it. If you have rejected glory, flee from those who hunt for praise. Flee from possessors as from possessions. Depart from those who live in luxury, as [you do] the luxuries. Flee from the lustful, as from fornication. If the memory of their way of life disturbs the mind, how much more so the sight of them and their proximity. Draw near to the virtuous that through them you may draw near to God.

85. Converse with the humble person that you may learn from his ways. If the sight of his way of life is useful to those who see it, how much more so the manner of his asceticism and the teaching from his mouth. Love the poor that through them you may find mercy. Do not draw near to the contentious lest you be constrained to go out from your peaceful habits. Do not flee from the foul diseases of those who are ill, because you also are clothed with flesh. Do not oppress the bitter in heart, lest you be struck with the rod with which they are beaten. Then you will seek a consoler and you will not find one. Do not despise the imperfect so as not to enter Sheol together with them.

86. Love sinners but despise their deeds. Do not treat them with contempt because of their faults, lest you

also be tempted by the same faults. Remember that you share in the stench of Adam, and you also are clothed in his infirmity. To the one who has need of ardent prayer and soothing words do not give a reproof instead, lest you destroy him and his soul be required from your hands. Imitate doctors who use cold things against fevers.

When you meet your neighbor force yourself to honor him beyond his measure. Kiss his hand and his foot and piously warm your heart with great love for him. Grasp his hands many times and place them on your eyes, and caress them with great honor. Attribute beautiful things to his person that are not his. And even when he is far away, speak good and beautiful things about him, calling him by special titles of honor. By these things and their like, not only will you constrain him to desire beautiful things, because he will be ashamed of receiving renown for what he has not really done, and thereby you will sow in him the seed of virtue; but also by these and similar ways to which you accustom yourself, you will establish in yourself peaceful and humble habits and be freed from many hard struggles, from which others acquire preservation by [ascetical] labors. And not only this, but also if that one who receives these honors from you has some defect or voluntary fault, when you show him it clearly, even with only a gesture, he will easily receive healing from you because he will be ashamed of your honor toward him and because of the demonstration of love that he sees in you constantly.

Keep this disposition toward all persons. And if you become indignant with anyone, and you burn with zeal for the sake of the faith or because of his evil works, or you accuse him or blame him, be attentive to your soul. We all have a just judge in heaven.[146] But if you have pity and seek to turn him to the truth, certainly you must suffer for his sake. And

---

[146]2 Tim 4:8.

with tears and with love you must speak a word or two to him, and not be enraged against him; you must even put away from your face any sign of hostility. Love does not know how to be angry; it is not enraged; it does not reprove passionately.[147] Wherever there is a sign of love and knowledge, there is profound humility from within the mind.

---

[147]Cf. 1 Cor 13:5.

SIXTH DISCOURSE

1. The fact that one is detected in accidental offenses shows the infirmity of nature, that our nature is necessarily receptive to this. It did not seem to God that it would be useful for a person to be completely raised above these infirmities before his nature arrives at the second creation.[148] And this receptivity to accidents is useful for subduing the mind. But to continue [transgressing] is impudence. There are three ways by which every rational soul may approach God: by ardent faith, by fear, by correction from God. For the order of love cannot be approached by itself alone, except by assuming one of these three modes.

2. As confusion of thoughts is generated by gluttony, so ignorance and confusion of mind [are generated] from intemperance in words and disorderly habits. The care of things disturbs the soul; and the attraction of works stirs up the mind, making it go out from silence and driving peace from it. The mind of the solitary who has engaged his soul in heavenly work ought to be without anxiety so that when he searches his soul and reflects, he will not see in it anything of this world nor any desire for visible objects. Thus, on account of his complete withdrawal from these passing things, he will be able to

---

[148]"Second creation" refers to the resurrection of the body, see Isaac, ch. 35 (Wensinck or D. Miller).

meditate night and day on the Law of the Lord[149] without any distraction. Labors of the body, without mental beauty, [are like] a barren womb and dry breasts. They do not bring [any] nearer to the knowledge of God. The body is wearied but those who labor in such a way are not concerned to uproot passions from their mind; so they reap and there is nothing.

As a man who sows among thorns and cannot reap, thus is the one who destroys his mind with anxiety and anger and greed for amassing riches, while sighing on his couch because of his many vigils and much abstinence. Scripture bears witness, saying: "As a people who did righteousness and did not forsake the judgement of its God, they ask of me judgement and righteousness and delight in drawing near to God. 'Why have we fasted and you have not seen it, and humbled ourselves and you did not know it?' Behold, in the day of your fast you do your own wills and sacrifices to all your own idols."[150] That is, instead of God, you hold evil thoughts and evil doctrines in your soul. To them you sacrifice daily the freedom you esteem. The sacrifice more to be honored than anything else, which you properly set apart for me, is that of your good works and inner devotion of the heart.

3. The soul which is purified by the thought of God in watchful vigil night and day is good earth[151] which makes its Lord rejoice by yielding a hundredfold. There the Lord will build on its foundations, round about it there will be a cloud for shade during the day and the brightness of a flame of fire, at night,[152] from within its darkness light will shine forth.[153]

4. As a cloud obscures the beams of light of the

---

[149]Ps 1:2.
[150]Is. 58:2f.
[151]Mt 13:8.
[152]Ex 13:21-22.
[153]Is 58:8.

moon, thus the vapour of the belly [conceals] the wisdom
of God from the soul. As a flame of fire on dry wood, so
is the desire of the body in a full belly. As oily material
provokes the heat of the flame, so delicacy of food
[provokes] carnal passion within the body. The knowledge of God does not dwell in a body that loves pleasures.
One who loves his body will not be deemed worthy of
divine gifts. As from birth-pangs fruit is born which
gladdens the one with child,[154] so from labors the knowledge of the mysteries of God is born in the soul. But to
the negligent and those who love pleasure, a fruit is
born causing shame. For as a father has pity on his son,[155]
so Christ has pity on a weary body and is near its mouth[156]
at all times. There is no price for the labor of wisdom.[157]

5. The stranger is one who in his mind has made
himself extraneous to all ways of this world. The mourner
is one who in this life spends all his days in hunger and
thrist and mourning for the sake of the expectation of
that heavenly hope. The solitary is one who, after placing
his habitation far from the sights of the world and
[looking] beyond, has only one request in prayer: the
desire for the future world. The riches of the solitary
life are either the consolation granted to one from the
midst of mourning or the gladness of faith that appears
in the treasury of one's mind. That person is compas-
sionate, who while exercising mercy, does not distinguish
in his mind one class of people [from another].

6. This is virginity: not only that a person guards his
body from the corruption of perverse follies, but that he also
have reverence for his soul even when he is alone.

7. If you desire chastity restrain the flow of base
thoughts by occupying yourself with the study of the

154Cf. Jn 16:21.
155Cf. Ps 103:13.
156Cf. Rom 10:8.
157Cf. Prov 3:13f; Wisdom 7:7f.

lections [of Scripture] and in continuous intercession before God. Then you will be armed within, against occasions [of sin] from nature. Otherwise you cannot discern
purity within yourself. If you wish to acquire mercy, first
train your soul to acquire contempt for things, lest their
weight draw the mind to forsake the enactment of its
anticipated purpose.

8. The limpidity of mercy is known from patience in
bearing injury, and the perfection of humility when it
rejoices in gratuitous slander.

9. If you are truly merciful, when you are wrongfully
and cruelly deprived of what is yours, you will not be
angry[158] within or without, and will not show your for-
bearance to others. Rather the damages of your oppression will be absorbed by passions of mercy, as the sharp-
ness of wine is tempered in much water. But show the
sign of limpidity [which comes from] great mercy, with
other things that you will add; and cheerfully do good
to those who do you wrong just as blessed Elisha did to
his enemies when they came to capture him.[159] By praying
and by blinding their eyes with phantoms, he showed
the power that was in him; and that if he so desired,
they would have been as nothing before him. But by
giving them food and drink and letting them go away,
he made known the mercy he possessed within himself.

10. If you are truly humble, do not be troubled
when you are accused falsely. Do not waste [your] breath
on the thing but actually take upon yourself the unjust
word [spoken] against you, while not being concerned
for yourself to persuade others that the matter is otherwise. Rather, ask forgiveness.

11. Others have taken on themselves of their own
accord, the hateful reputation of fornication.[160] Still others

158Cf. Mt 5:40.
1592 Kgs 6:18-22.
160See the example of St Macarius the Great, in Benedicta

have admitted to deeds of adultery of which they were
innocent. And the fruit of the sin which was not theirs,
they increased with tears as if it were theirs. And with
weeping they asked forgiveness of the false accuser for
sins not committed, while their soul was crowned with
all the perfect purity of chastity. Then others, so as not
to be praised because of the wondrous ways they were
keeping in secret, feigned the habits of madmen, though
they were stable with full discernment and tranquility.
And in amazement at the deeds, the holy angels declared
the greatness of persons such as these. But you profess
to be humble while others bear witness against themselves; and you do not endure in silence when things go
against you, yet you consider yourself humble. If you
are humble, examine your soul in these things, [to see]
whether or not you are troubled.

12. The many abodes in the house of the Father[161]
denote the mind of those who dwell in that place: that
is, the different gifts and spiritual levels in which they
take delight spiritually, and the diversity of the classes of
gifts. This is not because there is a distinction of dwelling
place with clear information of various places in particular
habitations, really set aside for each and every one himself. But rather that in one common use of this perceptible sun, to each and every one of us there is a particular advantage deriving from it according to the purity
of his vision. As when the inner part of the eye is able
to contain the diffusion of sufficient light, or as a lamp
in the same house divides the use of its light differently,
even though the lamp is not bereft of the simplicity of its
radiance by the many forms in which it appears.

So while they live in the same indivisible dwelling in
many distinct parts, to each person who has been con-

Ward, tr., *The Sayings of the Desert Fathers* (London: A. R.
Mowbray, 1975), pp. 105-106.
[161]Cf. Jn 14:2.

sidered worthy to be there, delight flows into his soul
from a unique intelligible sun at a set time, according
to the rank of his way of life, in one air and in one place
and one habitation, one vision and one way.

He who is inferior does not see the great measure of
the rank of his neighbor, as indeed he might be put to
shame by the many gifts of his neighbor and the paucity
of his own; and that this would then be to him a cause
of distress and mental torment, God forbid! It is not permitted to think things like these in that place of delights.
Each one delights within himself, in the gift he has been
deemed worthy of and in the dignity of his rank. But on
the outside, the vision for all is one, and the place is
one. And what is even truer, [each] will be as a kind of
dweller of angelic habitations in the unity of an aerial
place and in the equality of clear vision and with the
hidden awareness which belongs to their ranks in contemplative revelations that vary according to their ranks.

If indeed individual beings, apart from the activity of
the senses also [have] mental impulses, no one, not even
for the future world will dare with his word to declare a
way other than this, that is, the [difference depends] on
the intellect and on what follows [from it] though because of the perfection of nature [in the future world
this difference] be more evident. Therefore the word
spoken by the Fathers is true, that on the one hand there
is ignorance for an unrestricted time; on the other there
is limited time for the manifestation of the end of ignorance[162] together with the revelation of other particular
mysteries that are circumscribed in silence near the God-
head. For besides the highest place and the lowest posi-
tion there is no other place in the middle between this
and that in the future destiny. Either one belongs wholly
to the higher things or wholly to the lower ones. But

---

[162]Cf. Acts 17:30.

within this and that [one are] various degrees of recompense.

And if this true, as true it is, what indeed is that folly of men! Some of them say: I do not desire to be in the Kingdom; if only I can with diligence escape from Gehenna. Deliverance from Gehenna is the Kingdom. And falling from this is Gehenna. For the Scriptures have not taught us three places. What then [do they teach]? "When the Son of Man will come in his glory, he will set the sheep by his right hand but the goats by his left."[163] Not even here are three places spoken of but two: those of the right and those of the left. The differences between the places of their dwellings are distinct. And these, it says, "Shall shine forth like the sun in the kingdom of the Father."[164] And those [will go away] into everlasting fire.[165] Again, they will come from the east and from the west and will recline with Abraham and his sons in the kingdom.[166] But the sons of the promise who have not been obedient will go into the darkness outside of the kingdom. Here there will be weeping of the soul and gnashing of teeth[167] which is a suffering more grievous than fire. From this understand that desisting from the ascent is the torment of Gehenna.

It is beautiful for one to instruct sons of men to beautiful things and bring them with constant care from error to the knowledge of life. This is the rule of our Lord and his apostles and it is very exalted. But if one perceives in his soul that from friendly and constant contact such as this, his conscience languishes because of the sight of things and his tranquility of discrimination is disturbed and his knowledge darkened, since his mind still has need

---

[163]Mt 25:32-33.
[164]Mt 13:43.
[165]Mt 25:41.
[166]Mt 8:11.
[167]Mt 8:12.

of vigilance and greater subduing of the senses (for as
long as the senses are to be healed, he is sick; and while
he wants to heal others he loses the partial health of his
own soul and leaves the chaste freedom of his own will
for the tumult of the mind) let this one remember the
word of the Apostle which says: "Strong food is for the
healthy."[168] Let him turn his back lest he hear from them
as a proverb: How are you a physician for others, but full
of sores yourself?[169] Therefore let him keep to himself and
guard his own health only. Instead of perceptible words he
will perform the duties of a beautiful way of life. Instead
of the words of [his] mouth, others will be helped by the
health of his soul if he has been able to preserve it. Even
when he is far away they will be healed by his health, [that
is], by the zeal of his virtuous deeds. This is more excellent than his service to them with a plain word while he
himself was sick and in need of healing, he even more than
they were.

13.   For if the blind lead the blind, both will fall into
the pit.[170] "Strong food is for the healthy, and for those
whose senses are trained and strengthened to receive all
foods." This means [strengthened] against every attack
of the senses because the heart is healthy on account of its
training in perfection.

14.   When Satan wishes to defile the chaste mind with
thoughts of fornication, first he tempts its endurance with
vainglory since the beginning of this thought is not like
the beginning of the passions. He does this to a guarded
mind in which he is not easily able to put obviously bad
thoughts.

15.   But when he who is strong through the nourishment of the first thoughts,[171] goes out from his citadel and

[168]Heb 5:14.
[169]Cf. Lk 4:23.
[170]Mt 15:14.
[171]These are the thoughts which are good according to "nature"

goes away a little from there, Satan lays occasions of fornication on him while causing his mind to pass to lascivious things.

16. At first the mind is terrified by the sudden encounter with them because of the chastity of the thoughts that meets the things; for the mind which rules [the thoughts] has abstained from the vision of [such] things for some time. But then it is brought down from the height of its first thought, even if it is not defiled. And if it does not turn its back and ardently seize the first thoughts which are the cause of the second thoughts, when it meets often with these things, then custom will blind the discernment of the soul by the frequent meetings. Therefore according to the quantity and variety of the first affection, thus is subjection to the second.

17. To avert passions by memories of virtues is easier and also more beautiful than to conquer them in battle.

18. For when the passions go out from their place and are impelled to show themselves in conflict, then they also print forms and images in the mind. This order [of passions] possesses a great power to take strength from the mind, and the mind is greatly troubled and agitated. However, in the first mode that I mentioned, not even a trace of the passions may be recognized in the mind after their removal.

Bodily labours and meditation on Scriptures preserve purity. And labours are confirmed by hope and fear. Hope and fear are established in the mind by separation from others and by constant intercession. Until one receives the Paraclete, he needs written indications to fix profitable

---

in the Patristic understanding of nature: the healthy condition of man coming from the hands of his Creator, before sin. "Against nature" is everything which attacks this good health. "According to nature" is human life restored by grace to its original good health, reaching out in constant growth in the gifts of the divine life.

memories in his heart by means of images, to renew the
incentive for virtue by constant meditation on them, and
to see in his own soul vigilance against the subtle ways of
sin. For he does not yet possess the mighty power of the
Spirit, which drives out the forgetfulness that snatches
profitable memories from him, making him languish
through distraction of the mind.

19.   But when the power of the Spirit enters and dwells
in the intelligible powers of the pious soul, then instead
of laws that are [written] in ink, the commands of the
Spirit are fixed in the heart which the heart learns secretly
from the Spirit[172] without having need of the help of
sensible materials mediated by the senses.

20.   Whenever the mind learns from material things,
its learning is followed by error and forgetfulness. But
when its instruction is in those things which are incorrupt-
ible, its memory which is also not corrupted, will be
founded on their intelligible nature.

21.   There are good thoughts and there is a good will.
There are bad thoughts and there is a bad heart. But the
first [that is, thoughts], without the second [that is, will
and heart], are reckoned as less for recompense. [The
former] in fact are movements which pass within the mind
as the winds which pass in the sea lifting the waves. But
[the latter] are the roots; and recompense will be according to the disposition held by the foundation, good or bad,
and not according to the movement of thoughts. The soul
in fact does not cease from setting diverse thoughts in
motion. But if you reckon retribution for each of them,
although they have no root beneath, then a thousand times
a day you will be close to changing your benefits and your
sentence.

A young bird without wings is the mind that recently
has emerged from the tangle of passions by the labours

---

[172]Cf. Jer 31:33-34; 1 Jn 2:27.

of repentance. At the time of prayer it strives to raise itself above earthly things and it cannot. But it still creeps on the surface of the earth where the serpent crawls. And it concentrates its thoughts by means of reading and labours and fear and reflection on the kinds of virtue. For beyond these it does not know anything else. These things do keep the mind pure for a short time. But memories come again and disturb and defile the heart. For it does not yet feel the air of peace and freedom which holds the mind concentrated for a long time, while being tranquil without any memory of things. For it still has wings of flesh, that is, bodily virtues which are practiced openly. But it does not yet see and perceive the contemplation of those virtues which it practices, which are the wings of the mind by which it approaches heavenly things and journeys from the earth. As long as one serves God in a way perceived by the senses and with things, the impressions of the things are imprinted in his thoughts and his mind thinks of the things of God in corporeal forms. But when he perceives that which is within things, then according to the measure of his perception, his mind will also be exalted beyond the forms of things in due time. The eyes of the Lord are on the humble and his ears hearken to them.[173] The prayer of the humble one is as from his mouth to the ears [of God]:[174] May the Lord, my God, illumine my darkness![175]

When you are in stillness with the beautiful work of humility, when your soul is near to coming out from under thick darkness, this will be the sign to you: your heart will burn and glow as with fire night and day; so that you will consider all earthly things as ashes and dung. That is, you will no longer have pleasure

[173]Ps 34:15.
[174]Sir 21:5.
[175]Ps 18:29.

in touching food on account of the pleasure of the
new fervent deliberations which are continually being
moved within your soul. And suddenly a fountain of tears
will be given to you, so that tears will flow without constraint from your eyes like water from a torrent, without
constraint, while mingling with all your works. That is,
with your reading and with your prayer and with your
office and with your meditation and with your food and
with your drink—tears will be mingled with all that you
do. Therefore when you see these things in your soul,
take heart, you have passed through the sea. Increase your
labours and keep very vigilant, that grace may grow from
day to day. Until you encounter these things, your way
has not yet finally arrived at the mountain of God.[176]

If this [state] vanishes after you have found it, if that
fervour goes out without your being prepared to receive
another thing after this in exchange, woe to you [for]
what you have lost! Either you have exalted yourself or
you have been negligent. Now concerning what that is
which is appointed after tears, and what one encounters
after passing from them and what else there is after that
[state], we will describe below in those chapters on the
course of the ascetic life as something on which we have
been illuminated by the Scriptures and by the Fathers who
were entrusted with mysteries such as these.

22.   If you do not have the labours [of virtue], do not
speak of virtue. Afflictions for the sake of justice are more
precious to God than all vows and sacrifices. And the
fragrance of the sweat of these labours is more precious
than all the roots of sweet spices and fragrant herbs.

23.   Every virtue by which the body is not afflicted,
consider it an abortion without soul. Sacrifices of the just
are the tears of their eyes. And their acceptable offerings
are the sighs of their vigils. The saints call out because

---

[176] 1 Kgs 19:8.

of the burden of the body,[177] they sigh, and with grief
they send their prayers to God. At the sound of their cry
the holy hosts [of the angels] come to meet them to encourage them with hope and to console them.[178] The holy
angels are companions of the saints in temptations and
sufferings by being near them.

24. Labours and humility make man a god on earth;
but faith and mercy bring quickly to limpidity. Fervour and
a broken heart do not exist in the same soul, as also
those who are drunk do not have control of the mind.
When fervour is given, anxiety and mourning are taken
away. Wine has been given for gladness and fervour for
the joy of the soul.[179] The former warms the body. But
the word of God [warms] the mind. Those who are
kindled with fervour by applying the mind to hope are
ravished in their thoughts toward the future world. As
various phantoms of the imagination are before those who
are drunk with wine, so too that one who is drunk and
inflamed with future hope: he does not know distress, nor
the world, nor anything which is in it. Such things happen
to the simple of heart and fervent in hope.

These taste at the beginning of their way, by faith of
soul alone, the many things which will happen after long
labours of purification to those who proceed in the tradi-
tional way. All that the Lord wills, He does.[180]

25. Blessed are those who have directed themselves
simply and without investigation in the sea of tribulations,
in the fervour which is from God, and have not turned
their backs; for they will be quickly taken safely to the
port of promises, and will rest in those dwellings where
all who labour well will arrive. And they will be consoled

---

[177]Cf. Phil 1:23.
[178]Ps 34:8.
[179]Ps 104:15; Sir 31:28.
[180]Ps 135:6.

after their weariness and will exult in the joy of their hope. Those who run with hope are not occupied with seeing the injuries along the way, neither do they have time to investigate similar things. But when they have gone up from the sea, then [these things] are visible to them and they praise God for how they have been preserved in the midst of all those storms and many steep rocks of which they were not aware, because they did not care to make themselves look at similar things. But those who devise continuous opinions and want to become very wise, and apply themselves to seek solutions and to fear and to make many plans, and to see and reflect on the causes of the injuries and of unstable thoughts—such as these are usually found constantly at the door of their houses. The sluggard when he is sent out says: "There is a lion outside and murder in the marketplaces."[181] Or they are like those who said: "We saw giants there and we were as locusts in their eyes;"[182] and "their cities are strong, and their walls rise up to heaven."[183] These are those who at the time of death will find themselves at the beginning of their way. They are always becoming very wise but they never begin. But the simple one swims and crosses over with his first eagerness. He does not think of the body nor of the possibility that perhaps his ventures might not succeed.

Let not the greatness of your wisdom be a stumbling-block to you, nor a snare before you, [preventing you] from beginning valiantly and swiftly with hope in God on your journey which is sprinkled with blood,[184] lest you always be needy and naked of the knowledge of God.[185]

26. One who looks at the winds does not sow.[186] Better

---

[181]Prov 22:13.
[182]Num 13:32-33.
[183]Deut 1:28.
[184]Ap 19:13.
[185]Ap 3:17.
[186]Cf. Eccles 11.4.

for us is death in battle for the love of God than a life of shame and debility. When you are ready to begin [to practice] one of God's works, first make a testament as one who has no further life in this world and as one who prepares himself for death. Draw near to it by cutting off hope, as if indeed with that action your dissolution be completed, and your days be ended, so that you will not see many more days after that. Let this be firmly resolved in your mind, lest expectation of life deprive you of victory by being a cause of laxity in your mind. Therefore, do not allow wisdom to reign completely over your affairs. Make a little room in your mind also for faith. Remember always the days after death and laxity will never enter into your soul. As the word of the Sage, who said: "A thousand years in this world are not as one day in the world of the righteous."[187]

27. Begin valiantly every work of virtue; "do not approach it with a double heart."[188] In the course of your journey, do not doubt in your heart the hope of God's grace, lest you toil in vain and the labour of your work be a burden for you. But believe in your heart that God is merciful and that He gives grace to those who seek Him,[189] not according to our work but according to the love of our souls, and to our faith in Him. "As you have believed so it will be to you."[190]

28. [The following are the works of those who live in accordance with God.] Some knock their heads all day, this satisfies [the requirement] for the hours of their services. And there is a continual bending of one's knee which includes the number of one's prayers. There is a movement of tears which satisfies [the requirement] of

---

[187]Cf. Ps 84:11; 90:4.
[188]Sir 1:28.
[189]Cf. Ps 145:18-19.
[190]Mt 8:13.

one's canons and no one seeks anything besides it, because it is better than anything else. Some define the laws laid down for them by diligence in intellectual study. There is the suffering of hunger which consumes one's flesh and some are withheld from the completion of their work by the torments of the belly. Some in the mind's fervour do not interrupt their recital of the psalms. The heart of some burns with Scripture while others are captured by the meaning of the same. There are those whose lips are kept from moving in the ordinary way because of amazement for the verses [of Scripture]. Some have tasted all these things and are satisfied and turn back and desist. Others with only a few of these things are puffed up and [become] pompous and are led astray. Some are kept back from these things because of their own body, because of its many sufferings and pains; and some by all kinds of inducements: by power, by the praise of men, by passion for things, by habits of gluttony. But some serve well and stand firm and do not flee until they have taken possession of the pearl.[191]

29.   Joyfully begin every work which is for the sake of God. If you are pure of passions and of division of heart,[192] God will bring to completion and He will help you and make you wise; according to his will, and in a marvelous way, He will bring you to perfection.

To Him, glory and power and adoration and exaltation, forever and ever. Amen.

---

[191]Mt 13:46.

[192]For Isaac single-mindedness is the essence of the solitary life, it is "angelic work," to have "one thought for the Unique," p. 147 (Bedjam).

POPULAR PATRISTICS SERIES

1 *On the Priesthood* – St John Chrysostom
2 *Sermons from the Life of Saint John Chrysostom*
4 *Behold the Thief with the Eyes of Faith*– Late Antique Greek and Latin Sermons on the Good Thief
6 *On the Holy Icons* – St Theodore the Studite
7 *On Marriage and Family Life* – St John Chrysostom
8 *On the Divine Liturgy* – St Germanus
9 *On Wealth and Poverty* – St John Chrysostom
10 *Hymns on Paradise* – St Ephrem the Syrian
11 *On Ascetical Life* – St Isaac of Nineveh
12 *On the Soul and Resurrection* – St Gregory of Nyssa
13 *On the Unity of Christ* – St Cyril of Alexandria
14 *On the Mystical Life*, vol. 1 – St Symeon the New Theologian
15 *On the Mystical Life*, vol. 2 – St Symeon the New Theologian
16 *On the Mystical Life*, vol. 3 – St Symeon the New Theologian
17 *On the Apostolic Preaching* – St Irenaeus
18 *On the Dormition* – Early Patristic Homilies
19 *On the Mother of God* – Jacob of Serug
21 *On God and Man* – Theological Poetry of St Gregory of Nazianzus
23 *On God and Christ* – St Gregory of Nazianzus
24 *Three Treatises on the Divine Images* – St John of Damascus
25 *On the Cosmic Mystery of Christ* – St Maximus the Confessor
26 *Letters from the Desert* – Barsanuphius and John
27 *Four Desert Fathers* – Coptic Texts
28 *Saint Macarius the Spiritbearer* – Coptic Texts
29 *On the Lord's Prayer* – Tertullian, Cyprian, Origen
30 *On the Human Condition* – St Basil the Great
31 *The Cult of the Saints* – St John Chrysostom
32 *On the Church: Select Treatises* – St Cyprian of Carthage
33 *On the Church: Select Letters* – St Cyprian of Carthage

34 *The Book of Pastoral Rule* – St Gregory the Great
35 *Wider than Heaven* – Homilies on the Mother of God
36 *Festal Orations* – St Gregory of Nazianzus
37 *Counsels on the Spiritual Life* – Mark the Monk
38 *On Social Justice* – St Basil the Great
39 *The Harp of Glory* – An African Akathist
40 *Divine Eros* – St Symeon the New Theologian
41 *On the Two Ways* – Foundational Texts in the Tradition
42 *On the Holy Spirit* – St Basil the Great
43 *Works on the Spirit* – Athanasius and Didymus
44 *On the Incarnation* – St Athanasius
45 *Treasure-House of Mysteries* – Poetry in the Syriac Tradition
46 *Poems on Scripture* – St Gregory of Nazianzus
47 *On Christian Doctrine and Practice* – St Basil the Great
48 *Light on the Mountain* – Homilies on the Transfiguration
49 *The Letters* – St Ignatius of Antioch
50 *On Fasting and Feasts* – St Basil the Great
51 *On Christian Ethics* – St Basil the Great
52 *Give Me a Word* – The Desert Fathers
53 *Two Hundred Chapters on Theology* – St Maximus the Confessor
54 *On the Apostolic Tradition* – Hippolytus
55 *On Pascha* – Melito of Sardis
56 *Letters to Olympia* – St John Chrysostom
57 *Lectures on the Christian Sacraments* – St Cyril of Jerusalem
58 *The Testament of the Lord*
59 *On the Ecclesiastical Mystagogy* – St Maximus the Confessor
60 *Catechetical Discourse* – St Gregory of Nyssa
61 *Hymns of Repentance* – St Romanos the Melodist
62 *On the Orthodox Faith* – St John of Damascus
63 *Headings on Spiritual Knowledge* – Isaac of Nineveh
64 *On Death and Eternal Life* – St Gregory of Nyssa
65 *The Prayers of Saint Sarapion* – Saint Sarapion of Thmuis

ST VLADIMIR'S SEMINARY PRESS
1-800-204-2665 • www.svspress.com

We hope this book has been enjoyable and edifying for your spiritual journey toward our Lord and Savior Jesus Christ.

One hundred percent of the net proceeds of all SVS Press sales directly support the mission of St Vladimir's Orthodox Theological Seminary to train priests, lay leaders, and scholars to be active apologists of the Orthodox Christian Faith. However, the proceeds only partially cover the operational costs of St Vladimir's Seminary. To meet our annual budget, we rely on the generosity of donors who are passionate about providing theological education and spiritual formation to the next generation of ordained and lay servant leaders in the Orthodox Church.

Donations are tax-deductible and can be made at www.svots.edu/donate. We greatly appreciate your generosity.

To engage more with St Vladimir's Orthodox Theological Seminary, please visit:

www.svots.edu
online.svots.edu
www.svspress.com
www.instituteofsacredarts.com